W9-BQZ-762

THEMATIC UNIT
ANCIENT EGYPT

Written by Mary Ellen Sterling

Illustrated by Cheryl Buhler

Teacher Created Materials, Inc.
6421 Industry Way
Westminster, CA 92683
www.teachercreated.com
©1992 Teacher Created Materials, Inc.
Updated, 2001
Reprinted, 2004
Made in U.S.A.
ISBN-1-55734-292-X

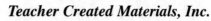

Table of Contents

Introduction

Ancient Egypt contains a captivating, whole-language, thematic unit about the way of life in ancient Egypt. Its 80 exciting pages are filled with a wide variety of lesson ideas and reproducible pages designed for use with intermediate and middle school children. At its core are two high-quality children's literature selections, *Pyramid* and *The Egypt Game*. For each of these books, activities are included which set the stage for reading, encourage the enjoyment of the book, and extend the concepts gained. In addition, the theme is connected to the curriculum with activities in language arts (including language experience and writing suggestions), math, science, social studies, art, music, and life skills (cooking, etc.). Many of these activities encourage cooperative learning. Suggestions for bulletin boards are additional timesavers for the busy teacher. Furthermore, directions for student-created Big Books and a culminating activity, which allow students to synthesize their knowledge in order to create products that can be shared beyond the classroom, highlight this very complete teacher resource.

This thematic unit includes the following:

- literature selections—summaries of two children's books with related lessons (complete with reproducible pages) that cross the curriculum

- poetry and drama—suggested selections and lessons enabling students to act out and create their own stories

- language experience and writing ideas—daily suggestions as well as activities across the curriculum, including Big Books

- bulletin board ideas—suggestions and plans for student-created and/or interactive bulletin boards

- homework—suggestions for extending the unit to the child's home

- curriculum connections—in language arts, math, science, social studies, art, and life skills

- group projects—to foster cooperative learning

- a bibliography—suggested additional books on the theme

To keep this valuable resource intact so that it can be used year after year, you may wish to punch holes in the pages and store them in a three-ring binder.

Introduction *(cont.)*

Why a Balanced Approach?

The strength of a whole-language approach is that it involves children in using all modes of communication—reading, writing, listening, illustrating, and doing. Communication skills are interconnected and integrated into lessons that emphasize the whole of language. Balancing this approach is our knowledge that every whole—including individual words—is composed of parts, and directed study of those parts can help a student to master the whole. Experience and research tell us that regular attention to phonics, other word attack skills, spelling, etc., develops reading mastery, thereby fulfilling the unity of the whole-language experience. The child is thus led to read, write, spell, speak, and listen confidently in response to a literature experience introduced by the teacher. In these ways, language skills grow rapidly, stimulated by direct practice, involvement, and interest in the topic at hand.

Why Thematic Planning?

One very useful tool for implementing a balanced language program is thematic planning. By choosing a theme with correlating literature selections for a unit of study, a teacher can plan activities throughout the day that lead to a cohesive, in-depth study of the topic. Students will be practicing and applying their skills in meaningful contexts. Consequently, they will tend to learn and retain more. Both teachers and students will be freed from a day that is broken into unrelated segments of isolated drill and practice.

Why Cooperative Learning?

Besides academic skills and content, students need to learn social skills. This area of development cannot be taken for granted. Students must learn to work cooperatively in groups in order to function well in modern society. Group activities should be a regular part of school life, and teachers should consciously include social objectives as well as academic objectives in their planning. For example, a group working together to solve a problem may need to select a leader. Teachers should make clear to the students the qualities of good leader-follower group interaction just as they would state and monitor the academic goals of the project.

Why Internet Extenders?

Internet extenders have been added to many of the activities in this book to enhance them through quality Web sites. This supplemental information helps to expand the students' knowledge of the topic, as well as make them aware of the many valuable resources to be found on the Internet. Some Web sites lend themselves to group research; other sites are best viewed by the entire class. If one is available, use a large-screen monitor when the entire class is viewing the Web site and discussing its content.

Although these Web sites have been carefully selected, they may not exist forever. Teacher Created Materials attempts to offset the ongoing problem of sites which move, "go dark," or otherwise leave the Internet after a book has been printed. If you attempt to contact a Web site listed in this unit and find that it no longer exists, check the TCM home page at *www.teachercreated.com* for updated URLs for this book.

Pyramid

by David Macaulay

Summary

*In **Pyramid**, David Macaulay provides the reader with a fascinating tour of an Egyptian pharaoh's burial tomb. After a brief introduction about life in ancient Egypt, the text quickly delves into the step-by-step construction of these magnificent man-made structures. The journey begins with a description of how the burial site was chosen and continues with the process of preparing for the actual building. Along the way we learn about construction tools and methods, types and functions of laborers, and interesting facts about life at that time. Black-and-white drawings enhance the text and act as references that help the reader visualize and understand the process as it is being explained. Completing the book is a glossary of terms employed throughout the pages. This book serves as a stimulating springboard for motivating students to learn more about pyramids and life in ancient Egypt.*

The outline below is a suggested plan for using the various activities that are presented in this unit. You should adapt these ideas to fit your own classroom situation.

Sample Plan

Day I

- Prepare a bulletin board (pages 74–77).
- Brainstorm; set up a file-folder system (page 6).
- Introductory film or readings (page 6).
- Assign pages 5–13 in Pyramid.
- Begin the Section Activities (page 10).
- Draw maps of ancient Egypt (pages 6 and 9).
- Knowledge and Comprehension (page 15).

Day II

- Assign pages 14–27 in *Pyramid*.
- Continue the Section Activities (page 10).
- History of Ancient Egypt on the Net (page 14).
- Flow Chart (page 17).
- Introducing Pyramids Using the Internet (pages 24–26)

Day III

- Assign pages 28–41 in *Pyramid*.
- Continue the Section Activities (page 10).
- Do Pyramid Math (page 19).
- Creative Writing Projects (page 20).

- Vocabulary Expanders (page 12).
- Knowledge and Comprehension (pages 15 and 16).

Day IV

- Assign pages 42–59 in *Pyramid*.
- Continue the Section Activities (page 11).
- Poetry Techniques (page 21).
- Vocabulary Game: Nefertiti (page 13).
- Egyptian Art (page 22).
- Math the Egyptian Way (page 28).
- Reading and Writing Hieroglyphics (page 27).
- Knowledge and Comprehension (page 16).

Day V

- Assign pages 60–79 in *Pyramid*.
- Complete the Section Activities (page 11).
- Construct paper pyramids (page 23).
- Learn about mummification (page 29).
- Meet the author (page 30).
- Bookmaking Ideas (page 31).
- Knowledge and Comprehension (page 16).

Overview of Activities

SETTING THE STAGE

1. **Assemble the King Tut's Mirror bulletin board** (for patterns and directions see pages 74–77) to spark student interest. Write the word "ankh" on the chalkboard. Encourage the students to research the symbolism and meaning of the ankh.

2. **Brainstorm with the whole class.** Discuss things that they know about Egypt. Have each student write his/her own list of what he/she knows about life in ancient Egypt. Staple each list to the inside of a file folder, write the student's name on the tab, and save the folder for future use. The file folders can be used to store samples of the students' work.

3. **Provide some background information about Egypt.** Tell the students to draw and label a map of ancient Egypt. Students can be paired to complete this activity freehand, or you may want them to use the ancient Egypt map on page 9.

4. **Introduce the topic of ancient Egypt with a movie.** Possible titles include *The Nile* narrated by Theodore Strauss (Warner Home Video, 1979) and *Anthony and Cleopatra* starring Charlton Heston (Embassy Home Entertainment, 1973). Keep in mind that any movie is a Hollywood interpretation. Preview any movies before showing.

   Check with your school district's media center, local and university libraries, and video stores for these and other titles.

5. **Burn incense, turn off the lights, and tell the students to relax.** Read aloud some excerpts from *The Book of the Dead*, a story from *Tales of Ancient Egypt,* or a short book such as *The Prince Who Knew His Fate* (see bibliography, page 80, for more information on these and other titles).

ENJOYING THE BOOK

1. **Assign a number of pages for reading each day.** See the Sample Plan on page 5 for suggested amounts. As students complete their assigned reading, reinforce the text with the Section Activities on pages 10 and 11.

2. **Vocabulary Expanders.** As students read the text, have them look for descriptive words, action words, and thematic words related to ancient Egypt. Record the words on an ongoing chart. Reinforce these words through any of the activities listed on page 12. (Suggested vocabulary words can also be found throughout the Section Activities on pages 10 and 11.)

3. **Nefertiti.** Older students enjoy games as much as younger ones. This word game is suitable and versatile enough to maintain their interest. Rules and directions are outlined on page 12. A sample written version of the game is contained on page 13. Note: Any thematic word can be used instead of Nefertiti. You may want to use "pyramid" or "King Tut," for example.

Overview of Activities *(cont.)*

ENJOYING THE BOOK *(cont.)*

4. **History of Ancient Egypt on the Net**—Page 14 is a great way to introduce students to the pyramids via the fascinating information found at the Web sites listed. Some of these are more appropriate for the entire class to see and discuss. Others may be assigned to student groups to research and then share with the class.

5. **Knowledge and Comprehension**—Use pages 15 and 16 as a study guide, review, or assessment tool. Work can be completed orally or written and may be done individually or in pairs.

6. **Pyramid Flow Chart**—The flow chart on Page 17 is another comprehension check. As an alternative way to present this lesson, write each step listed on a separate oaktag or construction-paper strip. Direct students to manipulate the strips in correct order from top to bottom.

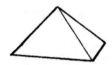

7. **The Funerary Complex**—This knowledge-and-comprehension check (page 18) can be used in conjunction with the Section Activity on page 10.

8. **Pyramid Math**—The 12 word problems on page 19 were derived from facts presented in Pyramid. They were designed to review basic math functions and to provide practice in employing math and critical-thinking skills.

9. **Creative Writing Projects**—Choose from 10 different writing assignments on page 20. Assign a different one each day or give students a choice from three or four that are presented to them.

10. **Poetry Techniques**—Review the cinquain on page 21. Model one with the students. Four additional poetry methods are also outlined on page 21. Incorporate vocabulary words in the poems as much as possible. Have the students highlight the vocabulary words they use with various colored highlighting pens.

11. **Art**—Have the students look at various ancient Egyptian artifacts. Discuss their observations. Establish the information outlined at the top of page 22. Select the art projects that are most appropriate for your students. Display the finished products in the classroom or arrange for a special display in the school library or entryway.

12. **Construct Paper Pyramids**—Supply each student with a copy of the pyramid pattern and construction directions on page 23. Assign any of the art, math, social studies, or language ideas that are given at the bottom of that page. Note: Let the students make construction paper pyramids using a template. To make a template of the pattern, copy it onto index stock and cut it out. Reinforce the outlines with a wide-tip marking pen. Have students trace around the shape onto a sheet of construction paper.

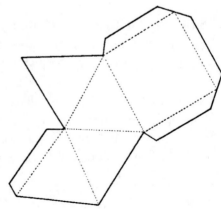

Overview of Activities *(cont.)*

ENJOYING THE BOOK *(cont.)*

13. **Introduce Pyramids using the Internet**—Fascinating information about the pyramids is available from the Web sites listed in the Internet Extenders on pages 24–26. Some of these Web sites are best viewed with the entire class as an overview of the topic. Two of the Web sites lend themselves to group research. Suggestions for the presentations are offered.

EXTENDING THE BOOK

1. **Visual Discrimination**—The ancient Egyptians developed an elaborate form of picture writing that used about 700 different signs. Scribes deliberately kept the system of hieroglyphics complicated to ensure their positions and to ensure that others could not master it. Challenge students to read the message on page 27, Reading and Writing Hieroglyphics. Use the Internet Extenders to learn more about hieroglyphics, including having students see how their names would appear in this language.

2. **Math the Egyptian Way**—Learn about the Egyptian system of numeration. A picture code is provided, and a number of math activities are outlined on page 28. Visit the Web site in the Internet Extender to help students create scale models of the pyramids.

3. **Mummification**—In order to complete the puzzle on page 29, students will have to research the topic. The embalming process is a fascinating story. It won't be difficult to motivate students to learn more about how Egyptians prepared the dead for the next world.

4. **Food Chart**—Draw Egyptian foods or cut out food pictures from magazines. Glue to a chart. Put a star next to those foods that students have eaten or are familiar with. Plan and prepare an Egyptian feast. Prepare and eat date cookies (recipe is on page 70), drink grape juice, locate more recipes on the Internet, etc.

5. **Meet the Author**—David Macaulay has written a number of books on some fascinating topics, including *Cathedral* and *The Way Things Work*. In addition, he illustrates his projects. Students will want to know more about this talented writer. See page 30 for his biography.

6. **Putting It All Together**—Culminate this section with a Big Book writing project. Directions for making a tiny book, shape book, and transparencies can be found on page 31. A number of suggested uses for each format are also supplied.

7. **Learn About the Seven Ancient Wonders of the World**—Fill in the chart on page 32. Visit the Web site in the Internet Extender to play a game of identifying these Wonders, applying the knowledge students have placed on their charts. Read *The Seven Ancient Wonders of the World* by Celin King (Chronicle Books, 1991).

Name_____

Ancient Egypt Map

The map below shows an outline of ancient Egypt. Learn more about this country by labeling the map with the following: Delta, Mediterranean Sea, Nile River, Red Sea, Lower Egypt, Upper Egypt. Color all bodies of water blue, the deserts tan, and the farmland green.

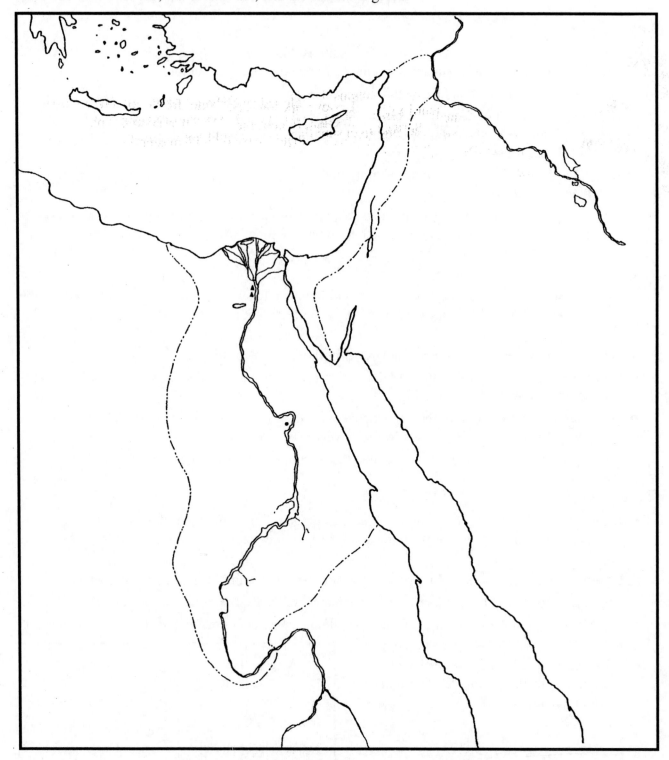

* Compare a current map of Egypt with the map above. Are there any changes?

Section Activities

Because the text is jam-packed with new vocabulary and technical details, you may want to divide the reading into manageable sections. Outlined below and on the next page are some suggested section-specific activities that may be utilized, changed, and adapted to fit your classroom program. A list of vocabulary ideas can be found on page 12.

Pages 5–13

- This pre-reading activity can be done in all sections: have the students explain in their own words what is happening in each picture. Read the text and compare explanations.
- On a map locate the Aswan Dam. Find out when it was built.
- Explain the function of each of the following parts of a typical funerary complex: valley temple, causeway, mortuary temple, boat pit, temenos wall, pyramid. (Optional: Have students complete the worksheet on page 18).
- Draw a cross section of a pyramid. Label the following: capstone, casing blocks, packing blocks, core blocks, and tomb.
- Vocabulary: inundation, receded, pharaohs, ba, ka, mastabas, Re, funerary, temenos, causeway, quarries, barracks, supremacy, compensation, remnants, mummification, theories, immortal

Pages 14–27

- Write a list of fifteen tools used by the pyramid builders. Draw a picture of each tool and describe its function. Compare these ancient tools to those used by builders today. Which ones are still in use?
- Write a step-by-step explanation of how true north was located. Illustrate each step.
- Construct a flow chart to explain the building process. As an alternative, have the students complete the flow chart on page 17.
- On a map find the location of the site where stone was quarried for the pyramid. An excellent resource is *Pharaohs and Pyramids* by Tony Allan, Usborne, 1977.
- Vocabulary: dolerite, rubble, scribes, oriented, horizon, arc, embedded, surveyors, symbolically

Pages 28–41

- Draw a floor plan of the tomb and the adjacent storage room. Label the following: sarcophagus, tomb, storage room, porticullises. In the storage room draw pictures of the pharaoh's most important possessions.
- Pretend you are the pharaoh. List your possessions that you would want to have buried with you.
- Create a cartoon strip to show how the sarcophagus was placed into the burial chamber.
- If you were to build a pyramid today, how would the construction method differ? Develop a chart to show these differences.
- Vocabulary: porticullises, sarcophagus, mortar, inscribed, friction, deterioration, corridor, barge, courses

Yesterday	Today
• Used primitive tools • Required thousands of workers	• Sophisticated machinery • Smaller work force needed

Section Activities (cont.)

Pages 42–59

- The pharaoh ordered a smaller pyramid for his wife. If you were pharaoh, how much smaller than yours would your wife's or husband's pyramid be? Draw pictures of both to show their relationship.

- Make your own plumb line. Tie a length of string to one end of a measuring stick. To the base end of the string, attach a washer or other weight. Use your plumbline to determine if pictures on the walls are straight.

- Farmers lived in mud houses. Find out what they were like and write a description of a typical Egyptian home. An excellent resource for this activity is *Ancient Egypt* (an Eyewitness Book) by George Hart (Alfred Knopf, 1990).

- After the capstone had been set in place, incense was burned and prayers were offered to the gods. Compose a prayer you might say if you were one of the priests at the ceremony. Burn incense to help set the mood.

- Vocabulary: summit, capstone, procession, preceding, perpendicular, plumblines, protruded, incense, dismantling, scaffolding, abrasive

Pages 60–79

- Draw and label a floorplan of the mortuary temple. Include the temenos wall, sanctuary, courtyard, storage, shrines, entrance hall, and causeway.

- Scenes of the pharaoh's journey into the next life were carved or painted on the facing stones. Find out how the painters were able to work in the deep, dark, tombs. *Exploring the Past: Ancient Egypt by George Hart* (Octopus Books, 1988) is a fine resource for this activity.

- Mummification was a complicated process which took about seventy days to complete. Learn more about the process by reading *Mummies Made in Egypt* by Aliki (Harper Trophy, 1979). Write a list of five fascinating facts you find.

- Write a paragraph explaining the significance of the "opening the mouth" ceremony.

- Vocabulary: sanctuary, successor, eternal, shrine, mummified, alabaster, embalmed, capitals, canopic jar, mastabas, relief carvings, anointed, resins, barge, conceal

More Ideas

- Assign students a number of pages to read daily. Have them write at least five important facts to know. Compile the facts on a master list and make copies for each student. Use the facts for reference and as a study aid. Note: You may want to divide the students into small groups or pairs for this activity. Also, compare lists before making a master sheet so that facts aren't repeated.

- Divide the students into small groups. Assign each group a different activity. Share their work in one large group.

- Give students a choice of activities. For example, tell students they must complete two of the four activities each day.

Vocabulary Expanders

On this page are a number of ideas that can be incorporated and employed to expand and reinforce vocabulary and spelling skills. Lists of suggested vocabulary words from *Pyramid* can be found in the Section Activities on pages 10 and 11. You may want to add or delete words to make the lists appropriate for your class. Choose the activities that best suit your teaching style, or give students choices from the activity list.

* List the vocabulary words on the chalkboard or the overhead projector for all to see. Instruct the students to look for the words as they read the text. Have them copy the sentence in which each vocabulary word appears. Next, tell them to rewrite each sentence, substituting a synonym for the vocabulary word.

* Begin an index-card dictionary. Assign each student a different vocabulary word. Tell students to write the word on an index card, define the word, and draw an illustration, if applicable. On the back of the card, write a sentence using the word. Add to the dictionary throughout the unit.

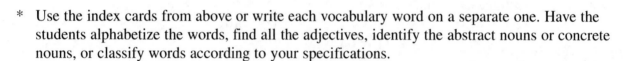

* Use the index cards from above or write each vocabulary word on a separate one. Have the students alphabetize the words, find all the adjectives, identify the abstract nouns or concrete nouns, or classify words according to your specifications.

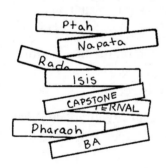

* Make vocabulary flash cards from strips of posterboard or index cards. Label each strip or card with one word. Write the corresponding definition on the back. Student pairs can practice quizzing one another. One partner supplies the definition or word while the other partner provides the answers. After all words have been defined, the partners change roles. Individuals can practice and self-check their own work.

* Write the vocabulary words on the chalkboard or chart paper; place the list where it will be visible. Direct the students to write a poem or creative story about ancient Egypt, using as many of the vocabulary words as they can. Highlight each vocabulary word used.

* Read other books and articles about ancient Egypt; see the bibliography, page 80, for some suggested titles. As the students read, direct them to look for the vocabulary words in the text.

* Substitute "Nefertiti" for vocabulary words in a sentence. Tell the students to refer to the list of vocabulary words on the board as you say each sentence. Have them repeat each sentence, using the correct vocabulary word. For example, you might say the following: "Transportation of the stones was easiest during Nefertiti." Students would respond: "Transportation of the stones was easiest during inundation." This can be done as an oral activity or a written exercise (see page 13).

12

Name_____

Nefertiti

Every time you see the word Nefertiti in the sentences below, cross it out and write the correct vocabulary word above it. Choose from the words provided at the bottom of the page.

1. The wooden coffin containing the pharaoh's mummy was placed in a Nefertiti.

2. Nefertiti contained the embalmed organs from a body.

3. The process of Nefertiti took seventy days.

4. Workers used Nefertiti to pound through granite and limestone.

5. Every year between July and November, Nefertiti would occur.

6. Egyptian kings were called Nefertiti.

7. Laborers built a Nefertiti around the entire base of the pyramid.

8. Egyptians believed that a person's Nefertiti lived on earth after death.

9. To prevent decomposition, Nefertiti was used to coat the corpse.

10. Nefertiti made of granite were lowered to seal the rooms after burial.

11. Because of gravity, the weighted string of a Nefertiti will hang perfectly vertically.

12. Light can be seen through Nefertiti, a very fine stone.

13. Topping the pyramid was a pyramid-shaped stone called a Nefertiti.

14. The Nefertiti contained a chapel and a small chamber for a statue of the deceased.

15. A person's Nefertiti traveled back and forth between the living and the dead.

ka	resin	mummification	ba
pharaohs	capstone	canopic jars	porticullises
alabaster	inundation	mastaba	sarcophagus
plumb line	temenos wall	dolerite	

History of Ancient Egypt on the Net

Use the following Internet Extenders to familiarize students with the history of ancient Egypt.

Internet Extenders

History of Egypt for Kids

http://touregypt.net/kids/History.htm

Activity Summary: A brief, illustrated history of Egypt appears at this Web site, especially appropriate for students in upper elementary and middle school grades.

History of Egypt

http://touregypt.net/ehistory.htm

Activity Summary: This Web site has links to descriptions of Egypt from the Lower Paleolithic (2 million–100,000 B.C.) to the British occupation period. Assign student groups to research the time periods you select and report their information to the class. Have the groups work together to summarize the important events of the periods they covered and develop a time line for the bulletin board. Additional information for this project may be gleaned from the time line Web site (below). This display may include a map of Egypt which can be derived from the follow Web site given below.

Timeline of Ancient Egyptian History

http://www.geocities.com/~amenhotep/history/index.html

Activity Summary: This interactive time line of the more than 3000-year-long history of ancient Egypt can provide additional information for the students as they do their research at the previous Web site. The time line begins with the Old Kingdom and extends to the Greek-Roman period. Extensive information is provided on each of these periods, including illustrations.

Map of Ancient Egypt

http://www.british-museum.ac.uk/egyptian/EA/further-info.html

Activity Summary: This map is divided into four sections, each of which can be enlarged by clicking on it. The map encompasses the Nile River area from the Mediterranean Sea to Aswan. Ancient cities along the river are marked. Print this map for display on the bulletin board.

Pharaohs of the Sun

http://www.british-museum.acuk/egyptian/EA/index.html

Activity Summary: This fabulous exhibition of ancient Egyptian artifacts consists of 250 objects from museums all over the world. You can see 20 highlights of this exhibit by clicking on view. When you reach the next Web page, click on the upper-left image to get more information related to it. You can click on the magnifier to get an enlarged view and then return to click on archival photos to see more details about this piece. Some pictures can be rotated or have short sound or video clips. Scroll down to the bottom of each Web page to see related objects and then click on them for more details. Click on the arrow in the upper right corner of the Web page to view the remaining objects. Several of the objects in this collection relate to the famous Nefertiti.

Knowledge and Comprehension

Assess students' knowledge and comprehension skills with the series of questions on this and the next page (16). Questions may be presented orally to the whole group for discussion or answers may be written by the students. For your convenience suggested answers are supplied in the 2nd column. The numbers in the parentheses indicate the pages on which the questions are based.

Questions	Answers
(5) What were the main occupations of the Egyptians?	Most were farmers; others raised cattle, sheep, goats.
(5) Explain what happened during the annual inundation.	Between July and November, the Nile rose and flooded the land.
(5) Describe the geography of Egypt.	Two narrow strips of farmland lining the Nile, desert to the east and west of the farmland.
(5) What did the ancient Egyptians believe about death?	It was the beginning of a new life in another world.
(5) What is the difference between the ba and the ka?	The ba continues to live on earth. The ka travels back and forth from the afterlife.
(5) Why were corpses mummified?	Eternal life depended on the ba and ka being able to identify the body.
(6) What were the two main functions of the tomb?	It protected the body from the elements and thieves, and it served as a house for the ka.
(6) What is the significance of the four triangular sides of a pyramid?	They represent the sun's rays shining down on the pharaoh and link him to Re, the god of the sun.
(6) In what way were the pyramids a failure?	They didn't protect the tombs from robbers.
(6) In what way were the pyramids a success?	They made their creators immortal.
(7) Who was Mahnud Hotep?	The pharaoh's architect and best friend.
(8) Why was the pharaoh's pyramid only to be 470' high?	To respect Khufu, builder of the largest Giza pyramids.
(11) What was the temenos wall?	A wall enclosing the area around the pyramid's base.
(11) Name the three main parts of the pyramid blocks.	The innermost section of core blocks, the packing and the casing blocks.
(13) Several thousand men were brought to the building site. What jobs did they have?	Stone cutters, surveyors, masons, mortar makers, carpenters, and general laborers
(13) Farmers were drafted during inundation; what was their function?	They were organized into gangs of 25 men to transport stone from the quarries to the building site.
(18) Why was transportation of the stones easier during inundation?	They could be transported by boat over the Nile.
(22) Why was it important to locate true north?	The pyramid had to be correctly oriented.
(25) Why were prayers offered and animals sacrificed at the pyramid site before construction began?	To ensure the gods' blessings over the project.
(25) Why were the connecting trenches filled with water?	It acted as a level.
(28) At what distance below the surface was the tomb?	Fifteen feet.

Knowledge and Comprehension *(cont.)*

Questions	Answers
(28) Name the granite doors used to seal the rooms.	Porticullises.
(30) Why were stones transferred to wooden rockers?	To make movement easier.
(30) Why were the stones numbered?	To indicate the order they needed to be placed in.
(30) What material was spread on the stones to ease friction?	Mortar.
(31) This is another name for outer coffin.	Sarcophagus.
(31) Why was the sarcophagus placed in the burial chamber before the roof was built?	It was too large to go through the tunnel.
(36) Overseers checked the work constantly. Why?	To prevent poorly finished surfaces from weakening the entire structure.
(38) Subsequent courses had to be raised to the top of the preceding one. How was this problem solved?	Mahnud Hotep built ramps of rubble and mud.
(38) Explain the purpose of logs embedded in the ramp.	They helped reduce deterioration.
(45) Why did surveyors use plumblines?	To ensure walls rose at the correct angle.
(46) When did pyramid bases become visible from afar?	By winter of the tenth year.
(48) For how many years was stone ferried?	14.
(50) Why were two ramps abandoned at 400 feet?	Not enough wall space for four ramps.
(52) How long had it taken to build 24 courses?	26 years.
(52) Name the granite block that rested on the top.	Capstone.
(56) How did the priests celebrate the capstone?	They burned incense and offered prayers to the gods.
(58) What was used to polish the capstone?	Pieces of stone and abrasive powder were used.
(60) What was contained in the mortuary temple?	Entry hall, courtyard, 5 shrines, a sanctuary with a false door, and storage rooms.
(62) What did workers paint on the facing stones?	Scenes of pharaoh's journey into the next life.
(64) Describe mastabas.	Tombs built around royal buildings.
(66) What was the purpose of the oblong pits?	Housed boats for pharaoh's use in afterlife.
(69) How was the interior passage illuminated?	By slots in the roof.
(70) What happened to the royal barge after the body was removed?	It was dismantled and placed in the remaining pit.
(72) Explain how the brain was removed.	It was dissolved with a special liquid and then pulled through the nose with hooks.
(72) What was done with liver, lungs, and stomach?	They were embalmed and put in canopic jars.
(75) Explain the significance of the "opening the mouth" ceremony.	It symbolically restored pharaoh's ability to eat, speak, and move.
(77) What objects filled the burial chamber and the storeroom?	Food, clothing, furniture, jewelry, weapons, and games.
(79) How many blocks of stone were used in the construction of the pharaoh's eternal home?	More than two million.

Name_____

Pyramid Flow Chart

As soon as the plan for the pyramid was approved, construction could begin. Write the steps listed below in the correct order on the pyramid.

*The men rolled the stone block onto a wooden sled. *Tunnels were dug into the face of the cliff. *The land was cleared. *The stone block was dragged to a waiting boat. *Scribes prepared a list of necessary stone. *The work gang's name was checked off the list once they reached the site. *Work orders and lists of stones were sent to the quarries. *Each block was cut and assigned to a work gang for delivery.

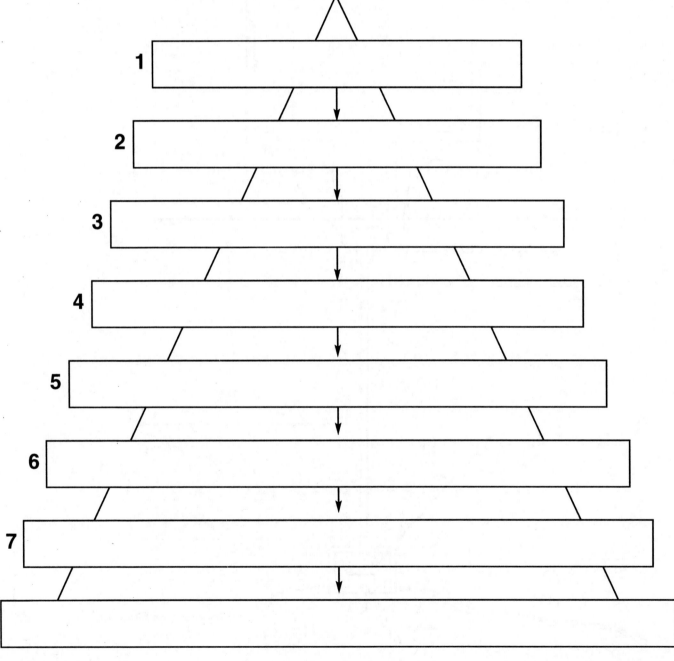

Name_____

The Funerary Complex

Below is a floor plan of a funerary complex. First, label the structures. Then explain the function of each on the lines provided.

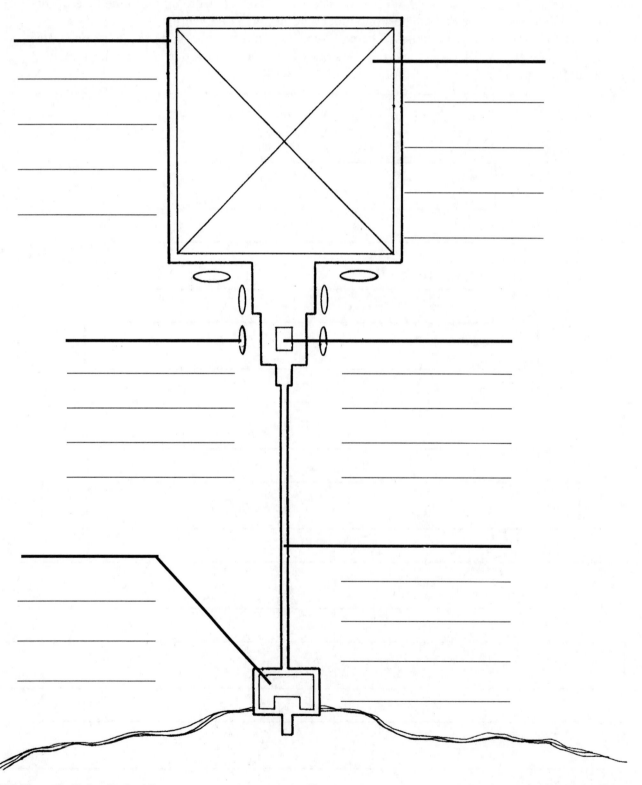

Name_____

Pyramid Math

The word problems on this page are based on facts from David Macaulay's *Pyramid.* Work alone or with a partner to solve each one. Write your answers on the lines provided.

1. _____ The pharaoh's pyramid was 470 feet (143 m), which was 10 feet (3 m) lower than Khufu's. How tall was Khufu's pyramid?

2. _____ For nine months of the year farmers tended their crops. What fraction of a year did they farm? Reduce the fraction to its lowest terms.

3. _____ Between 3000 B.C. and 1100 B.C. Egypt was ruled by a long line of pharaohs. How many years did the pharaohs rule altogether?

4. _____ A work force of 50,000 farmers was drafted to work on the pyramids each year. They were divided into gangs of 25. How many gangs were created?

5. _____ Each side of a pyramid was 740' (225 m) long. How many feet (meters) was it around the base of the pyramid?

6. _____ In November 2468 B.C. the pyramid site was marked, but it wasn't leveled until the end of September 2467 B.C. How much time had passed?

7. _____ One hundred twenty-four courses had been completed in 26 years. Approximately how many courses were built each year? Round to the nearest whole number.

8. _____ A second royal tomb was begun in 2461 B.C. The first had begun in 2468 B.C. How many years passed between the construction of the two tombs?

9. _____ Two million stones were used in the construction of the pharaoh's eternal home. Write the numeral for two million.

10. _____ Granite was found 600 miles south in the Aswan. How many kilometers is that? (1 mile = 1.6 km)

11. _____ Stones in the first course were moved easily, but the next 123 courses had to be raised on top of the preceding one. How many courses were there altogether?

12. _____ In 2457 B.C. work gangs began quarrying at Tura. For the next 14 years, they ferried stone across the flooded valley. In what year was the process completed?

Creative Writing Projects

Motivate students with the following creative-writing projects and ideas. Before beginning some of the activities, though, you may want to conduct a brainstorming session or model the assignment. Share the finished products in small groups, class scrapbooks, or display them on the walls or special bulletin boards.

1. Experiment with alliteration. Since Ps are plentiful, that might be a good place to start. Write alliterative sentences such as: Papyrus pyramids protruded perpendicularly. Refer to the vocabulary words on pages 10 and 11 for more possibilities.

2. A time machine has enabled you to go back in time to ancient Egypt. Write a story about what you see and do while you are there. Unfortunately, you only have forty-eight hours to investigate the old world.

3. Write an ABC book of Egypt for younger students. Include a brief description and an illustration, as well as the word, on each page. If desired, use a tiny book format (see page 31) for this project; divide the alphabet among groups.

4. You are in training to be a scribe like your father. However, you would rather be outside playing with other children. That night you decide to have a talk with your father to tell him you no longer want to study. Write the conversation that the two of you might have. Keep in mind that you are in ancient Egypt. Next, rewrite the conversation as if it were to take place today.

5. Compare two different things using *like* or *as*. For example, "In the hot sun, the desert glistened like the water of the Nile." Write five similes. Choose words related to ancient Egypt.

6. Write a how-to book about building a pyramid. Be sure to include a step-by-step outline of the process along with illustrations.

7. Girls in ancient Egypt did not go to school. They stayed at home and learned what they needed there. Write a story about a girl's typical day at home.

8. Design a flip book that describes how to mummify a body, how the stones for the pyramids were quarried and shipped to the building site, or how to make papyrus.

9. The Egyptians had no money. How would your life change if there were no more money in the world and you had to barter for your video games, makeup, clothes, etc.? Write a story about how you would cope with this crisis.

10. Write rhyming couplets. Read through a vocabulary list to find rhyming words. Then write two rhyming lines. An example follows:

    The ka returned to its mummy at night.
    By spreading its wings and taking flight.

Poetry Techniques

Students will enjoy writing with these creative techniques. Model them for the students if they are unfamiliar with a particular format.

Cinquains

A cinquain consists of five lines all reflecting on one topic. Each line must be written according to specific rules. A sample cinquain appears at the right below.

Line 1: the subject, which must be a noun

Line 2: 2 adjectives that describe the subject

Line 3: 3 action verbs that end in "ing" and describe the subject

Line 4: a phrase or sentence that describes the subject

Line 5: a synonym for the subject, also a noun

Pharaoh
powerful, dignified
reigning, decreeing, watching
a god to his people
King

Title Poem

Nebulous and notorious
It rises and falls regularly
Leaving behind fertile
Earth for planting

Write the subject of the poem down as shown at left. Then use the letters that spell the name of the subject to begin each line. The words should convey a single thought.

I Wish I Were

Have the students begin the first lines of their poems with, "I wish I were." After they complete the first line, direct them to write a second rhyming line. Two examples follow.

I wish I were the god Osiris.
I'd write my name on sheets of papyrus.

I wish I were the ancient Sphinx.
Looking out on a world that sometimes stinks.

Alphabetical Poem

Choose a title for your poem. Then beginning with the letter A, write a descriptive word for your subject. Write an adjective using the remaining letters in alphabetical order. For example:

Egypt

Ancient, barren, cultured, desert, eternal, fertile, great, honorable, inventive, judicious, kindly, laudable, memorable, noble, organized, proud, quaint, religious, sacred, tenacious, unassuming, valuable, wealthy, exact, yearning, zealous.

Free Form

Turn off the lights, burn some incense, and relax. Have students invent their own forms of poetry. With the whole group, share the new forms of verse.

The Character of Egyptian Art

Display pictures of ancient Egyptian artwork or direct students to find examples in their textbooks. Discuss the characteristics of the art. Establish the following:

1. Egyptian art was largely influenced by people's beliefs about religion and the afterlife as evidenced by their scrolls, tombs, pyramids, and statues.

2. Several distinguishable characteristics can be found in Egyptian art. Note how the upper body is shown from the front while the lower body is shown from the side. Women are painted a lighter shade than the men. Slaves and servants are drawn smaller than people who were considered more important.

3. Through their art we have come to learn and understand the Egyptian way of life.

As a follow-up to the discussion, select one of the art projects below.

Profiles

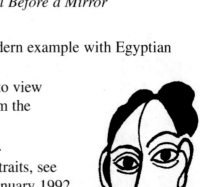

Materials: pencils; paper; tape; opaque projector (optional)

Directions:

• Pair the students. Have them take turns drawing a profile of one another with an opaque projector (see illustration above right) or freehand.

• Direct the students to fill in their outlines with eyes, neck, hair, etc.

Picasso

Materials: mirror; pencil or art chalk; paper; picture of Picasso's *Girl Before a Mirror*

Directions:

• If possible, study a print of *Girl Before a Mirror* which is a modern example with Egyptian influence.

• Tell students to look at their faces in a mirror. Encourage them to view themselves from various angles. Or, they can use the mirror from the bulletin board (pages 74–77).

• Have them draw a stylistic self-portrait based on Picasso's style.

• **Note:** For those who are interested in making computerized portraits, see the article "Graphic Self-Portraits" on pages 16 and 17 of the January 1992 issue of *School Arts* magazine.

Decorative Coffin

Materials: picture of an Egyptian coffin; drawing paper; colored pencils or pens; scissors

Directions:

• Tell the students to draw an outline of a coffin by tracing over a picture of one or sketching it freehand.

• Have them decorate the coffin with words, pictures, and symbols that they think will tell people about themselves.

• Cut out the coffins and display.

• Give students a chance to identify each coffin before labeling each with the artist's name.

Pyramid Pattern

Construct paper pyramids following the directions below. Use the pyramid for any of the activities outlined at the bottom of the page.

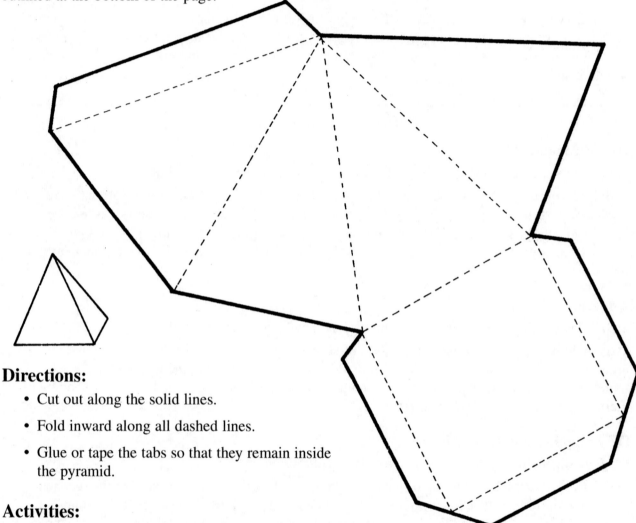

Directions:

- Cut out along the solid lines.

- Fold inward along all dashed lines.

- Glue or tape the tabs so that they remain inside the pyramid.

Activities:

Before gluing or taping the tabs, do the following:

1. Draw a message in hieroglyphics on each triangular face.

2. Decorate the faces with a variety of amulets.

3. Draw a different god or goddess on each face. Write a sentence about his or her function.

4. Write a different vocabulary word on each face. Define and illustrate the words.

5. Compose a four-line poem. Write a separate line on each face.

6. Measure the sides of the base. What pattern do you see? (The sides are equal in length.) What geometric figure is it? (square) Measure the triangles. Is one larger than the others? (No; in fact, they're all the same.) How many degrees are in each angle?

7. Write a riddle. On each face write a different clue. Write the answer to the riddle on the base. For example, "My name is simple. Some call me a soul. I'm part bird. I return at night." Answer: "Ba."

Pyramid

Introducing Pyramids Using the Internet

Use the following Web sites to introduce the study of pyramids to the class. If available, use a large computer monitor so the entire class can work together reading and discussing the content. This will establish a foundation for student groups visiting the other Web sites in this series. They will gather information and then present this to the class.

Internet Extenders

Map of Saqqara North

http://www.geocities.com/~amenhotep/topo/saqqara/main_topography_2.html

Activity Summary: This is a "clickable" map that leads to further information regarding some areas shown. Print a copy of this map and then make a transparency of it to use as a reference during visits to the following Web site. You may prefer to return to this map on the computer as you cover the pyramids described at the related Web sites below in order to provide orientation for the various pyramids.

Saqqara, City of the Dead

http://www.geocities.com/~amenhotep/topo/saqqara/main_topography.html

Activity Summary: Saqqara-North consists of several smaller cemeteries that grew around the larger monuments. Visit this Web site to provide information regarding the location and importance of this area. The "clickable" map located on this Web page may be used now or later after going to the related Web sites shown below.

The Pyramid Complex of Djoser

http://www.geocities.com/~amenhotep/topo/saqqara/djoser.html

Activity Summary: The building of the step pyramid and surrounding complex for the second king of the third dynasty, Djoser, represents a dramatic leap forward in the ancient Egyptians' mastering of architecture and technology. Prior to Djoser, the materials used for building temples and funerary complexes were mostly mud bricks and wood. With Djoser's complex, the Egyptian builders, under the direction of the architect Imhotep, moved to using more solid materials.

This is the first of seven Web pages on the Pyramid Complex, using photographs and text to cover the topic. When you have finished visiting this first one, scroll down to the bottom list at each of the Web pages and click on the following sequence of links.

(2) Entrance   (5) North Temple/Sedab

(3) South Court   (6) South and North Houses

(4) Pyramid   (7) Heb-Sed Court

Researching Pyramids on the Net

Use the first two Web sites with the entire class as an introduction. Divide the students into two groups. Assign one to do the Pyramid Tour and the other The Sphinx (page 26).

Internet Extenders

The Dig at Giza

http://www.pbs.org/wgbh/nova/pyramid/explore/gizahistory.html

Activity Summary: Read about this dig at the first Web site and then read the interview of the archaeologists and director of the dig at the second.

Pyramid Tour

http://www.pbs.org/wgbh/nova/pyramid/explore/

Activity Summary: Follow the instructions below to explore the pyramids.

1. Click on "Khufu" to see a picture of the exterior of this pyramid.
2. Click on the smaller picture to see the view from the top. Can you see its shadow? Read the interesting information and then click "Back to Khufu's Pyramid."
3. Look at the cross section of this pyramid and read the captions to help you find your way around inside it. Click on "Inside Story."
4. Read the information about King Khufu, father of pyramid building. Read the information and print a copy of the cross-section drawing. This drawing will help you as you tour the pyramid and can be used in your presentation.
5. Now, read the warning on this Web page. If you are brave enough, click on "ENTER HERE" to begin touring the pyramid.
6. Click on "Photographic Route" to take a 360-picture tour. Look at the picture of the entrance and locate exactly where you are by looking at the circle on the map. Find this location on the drawing you printed and circle it.
7. Navigate your way through the pyramid, clicking on underlined locations beneath each picture. Always check where you are on the printed drawing.
8. What happens when you click on "Out of the Pyramid?" Once you have discovered the surprise, reenter the pyramid and click on "Back to Enter Here."
9. Use the following instructions to help with your presentation.

   - Print copies of each of the chambers you visited. Write captions for each picture in your own words. Include the information you learned about each area and impressions you had as you took the tour.
   - Make an enlarged copy of the cross-section map of the pyramid. Place the map in the center of a bulletin board and the pictures around it. Connect each picture to its location on the map with string.

Researching Pyramids on the Net *(cont.)*

Internet Extenders

The Sphinx

http://www.pbs.org/wgbh/nova/pyramid/explore/sphinx.html

Activity Summary: Follow the instructions below to learn about the Sphinx.

1. Click on "Restoring the Sphinx" and read the interview with Dr. Zahi Hawass, Director of the Pyramids. Print a copy of this interview to use as a reader's-theater script to present to the class. Print colored copies of the photographs and then make transparencies of them to use during your presentation.

2. Click on "Inside Story" and then read information about the Sphinx. Create a presentation of this information for the class. Include printing a color picture of the Sphinx if possible. Show the dimensions of the Sphinx by cutting strings the length and height of the Sphinx. Do the same for the width and height of the head. Tie cards on the strings and write the length and Sphinx part on each card. Next, take the class out to a field or playground and lay out the strings. Show the picture to help everyone get a better idea of what the Sphinx looks like.

3. Use one computer with a large screen, if available, and do the following activities with the entire class during your presentation.

   • Click on "QTVR Sphinx" to see spectacular views of the Sphinx from different views and distances. If you have the plug-in Quick Time, it can be used to activate the photograph of the Sphinx on the left.

   • Place the cursor on this picture, and it becomes a hand. Click and hold the closed hand and pull it left or right to rotate the Sphinx. Stop at various positions and use the (+) or (-) below the photo to zoom in or out. Use the two people as a size reference for the Sphinx.

   • Click on "Back" to look at the map and find which pyramids are shown near the Sphinx.

The following Web site should be shared with the entire class after all of the presentations are completed.

Khafre Pyramid

http://www.pbs.org/wgbh/nova/egypt/explore/khafre.html

Activity Summary: The plug-in Quick Time activates the picture of the pyramid. First scroll down to the picture of visitors on the camel to get information about what you are seeing in the picture. Place the cursor on the picture, click, and hold it to slowly rotate it. Release the mouse button to stop and zoom in on any part of the picture. You can also move up and down. Click on "Back" to return to the map to help put the views back in perspective.

Reading and Writing Hieroglyphics

Use the code in the key below and the clues given to translate the message below. Write the words on the lines provided. Hint: Some words are pictured phonetically, so letters may be missing.

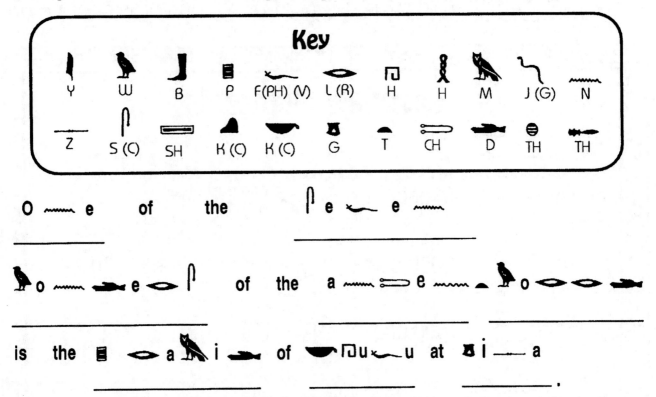

Internet Extenders

Hieroglyphics

http://www.pbs.org/wgbh/nova/pyramid/hieroglyph/

Activity Summary: Have the students read the first two Web pages and then print the third, which contains a message in hieroglyphics to be decoded, along with the alphabet in hieroglyphics. Divide the students into small groups and then let them complete the task of decoding the message, sharing their results, and then checking them with the last Web page at this site.

Your Name in Hieroglyphics

http://webperso.iut.univ-paris8.fr/~rosmord/nomhiero.html

Activity Summary: When you reach this Web site, look for the space in which to type your name. After doing this, click on "Send" to see what your name looks like in hieroglyphics. Check the names of family members and friends. Make prints of these names to give to them.

Hieroglyphics

http://emuseum.mankato.msus.edu/prehistory/egypt/hieroglyphics/hieroglyphics.html

Activity Summary: This Web site includes a different version of the alphabet. It also has a lengthy but very interesting history of the demise of hieroglyphics and its revival with the discovery of the Rosetta Stone.

Math the Egyptian Way

Introduce students to the numerals used by the ancient Egyptians. Make a copy of the chart below for each student, make an overlay for the overhead projector (see how to on page 73), or enlarge the chart (for an easy method see page 31) so it may be easily viewed. Use any of the math activities listed at the bottom of the page or create your own projects.

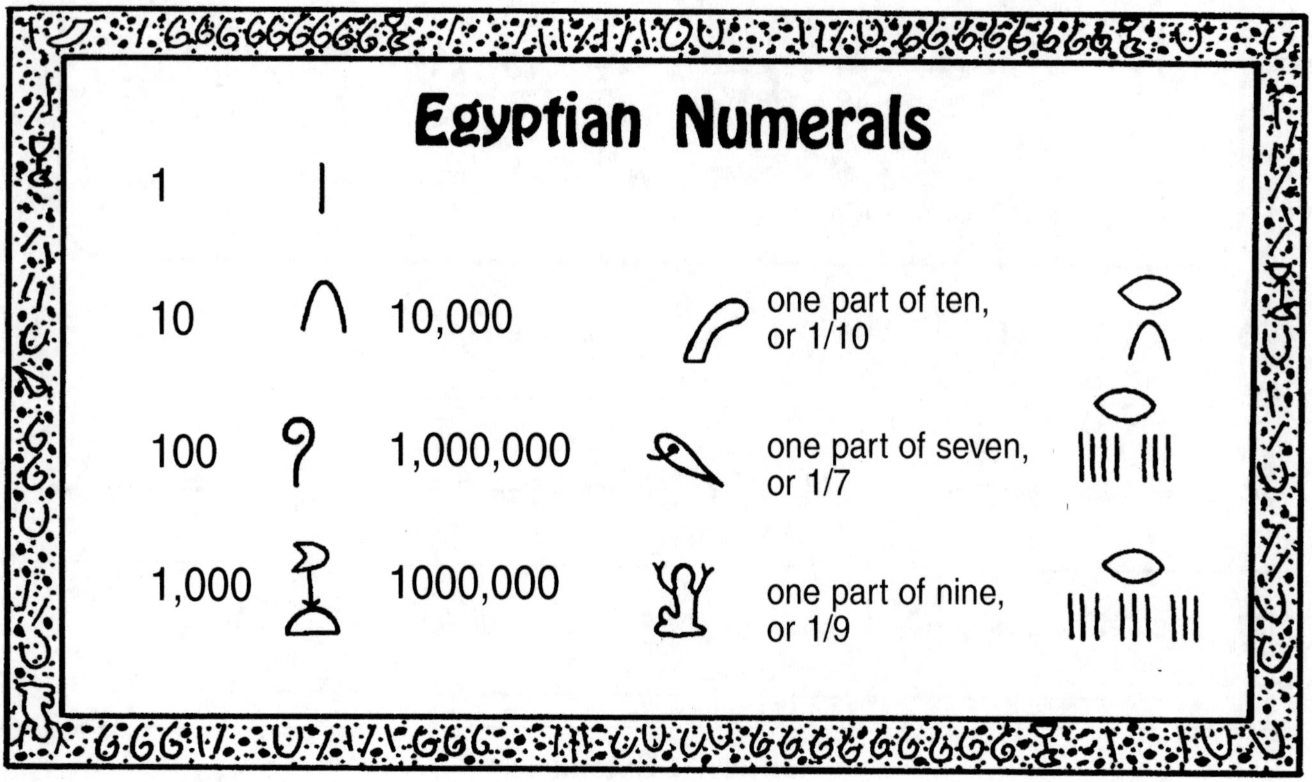

Math Activities

- Direct the students to write their birth dates using Egyptian numerals.
- Write the Egyptian fractions for 1/7, 1/6, and 1/10 on the chalkboard or overhead projector for all to view. Ask students to identify the pattern. Have them write fractions for 1/2, 1/3, 1/4, 1/5, 1/6, 1/8.
- Tell the students to write all the numerals from one to one hundred using Egyptian numerals.
- Make a class-sized poster or bulletin board of the numerals from one to one hundred, using Egyptian numerals.

Internet Extender

Make a Scale Model of the Pyramids

http://www.pbs.org/wgbh/nova/pyramid/geometry/

Activity Summary: First, explore the Great Pyramid shown at this Web site by clicking on its dimensions. Here you will discover its height and how it compares to other structures. Determine how many "refrigerators" an average block in the Pyramid would weigh. Compare the base to the size of a football field. Finally, construct a scale model, using the printout provided for you. The final challenge is to construct scale models of two other pyramids, using the information you will find at this Web site.

Name _____

The Mummification Process

Learn more about the mummification process.

Read reference books and other resources to find the answers to the following clues. Then write the words in the puzzle below.

1. This substance was used to stuff the nostrils.
2. Besides human beings, Egyptians embalmed these.
3. Fingernails and toenails were covered with this precious metal.
4. This god guarded the liver's canopic jar.
5. He was Prince of the Dead, God of the Underworld.
6. This chemical was used to embalm the organs.
7. Portrait masks were often made of this material.
8. This collection of spells was buried with the mummy.
9. This fabric was used to plug the eye sockets.
10. These magical figures were placed in between layers of the mummy's wrapping. _____
11. This picture writing was used by ancient Egyptians.
12. These mummy-shaped figures worked in the afterlife's fields for the mummy. _____

* Two excellent resources for this activity are *Mummies Made in Egypt* by Aliki (Harper Trophy, 1979) and *Ancient Egypt* (an Eyewitness Book) by George Hart (Alfred A. Knopf, 1990).

Meet the Author

A natural extension activity to follow-up the reading of *Pyramid* is to learn about the author/illustrator David Macaulay. Some vital statistics are outlined below to give a bit of background information about the man behind this captivating text. Suggested student projects follow.

Résumé

Name: David Alexander Macaulay

Birth Date: December 2, 1946

Birth Place: Burton-on-Trent, England

Parents: James (textile machine designer) and Janice Michel (organist and choir director)

Children: One daughter

Education: Went to grade school in England until 1957 when the family moved to Bloomfield, New Jersey. Five years later they relocated to Rhode Island where he completed his junior and senior years of high school. Attended the University of Rhode Island where he studied architecture, engineering, and bridge building.

Career: Taught junior high school. Worked in an interior design office. Worked as a freelance illustrator of children's books during which time he began to write his own books.

Books: *Cathedral: The Story of Its Construction* (Houghton Mifflin, 1973); *City: A Story of Roman Planning and Construction* (Houghton Mifflin, 1974); *Pyramid* (Houghton Mifflin, 1975); *Castle* (Houghton Mifflin, 1977); *Underground* (Houghton Mifflin, 1976); *The Way Things Work* (Houghton Mifflin, 1973)

Awards: *Cathedral:* one of the Ten Best Illustrated Books by the New York Times, a Caldecott Honor Book, and a Children's Book-Showcase title (both 1974); *City:* a Children's Book Showcase Title (1975); *Pyramid:* the Christopher award, an Outstanding Book of the Year by the *New York Times*, (1975) and a Boston Globe-Horn Book, honorbook (1976); *Underground:* Outstanding Children's Book of the Year by the *New York Times* (1976); *Castle:* Caldecott Honor Book, Boston Globe-Horn Book honor book, honorable mention from New York Academy of Sciences Children's Science Book Award (all 1978).

Projects:

- You have been chosen to interview Mr. Macaulay for your school newspaper. What questions will you ask him?

- Read another book written by David Macaulay. Compare it with *Pyramid* in a Venn diagram.

- Write and illustrate your own architectural book. Possible titles might be *House* or *Shopping* Mall.

- The awards listed in the resume are only a few that Macaulay has received for his work. Find out what other awards he has been given.

Putting It All Together

As a culminating activity, students can write a book. Three different formats and a variety of writing ideas are explained below.

Tiny Books

Materials: butcher or notebook paper; colored pencils or pen; scissors

Directions:

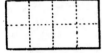 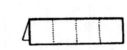

1. Fold paper to make 8 boxes.
2. Fold in half; cut slit to 1st fold only.
3. Open up. Fold along long fold.
4. Push both ends toward middle.
5. Push until middle is flat.
6. Fold sides over in the same direction.

Suggested Uses: Make alphabet books (see page 20), a mini dictionary of Egyptian terms, or a picture story for younger students. Create your own Egyptian code book.

Enlarged Shapes

Materials: pictures of Egyptian art; tracing paper; marking pen; opaque projector; tape; pencil; poster board or butcher paper; scissors

Directions:

- With the black marking pen, trace the outline of the picture.
- Tape a large sheet of poster board or butcher paper to the wall.
- Use an opaque projector to display the pattern onto the paper.
- Trace with a pencil. When the outline is completed, retrace with the marking pen and cut out.

Suggested Uses: Write a creative story about *The Last Mummy in Egypt* or *The Mummy Who Came to Life*. Write a series of poems within the shape. Write "how to" directions; for example, on a pyramid shape write directions explaining how to make a pyramid transparencies

Materials: acetate sheets or overhead transparencies; marking pens

Directions:

- Group the students. Have each group write their own original story.
- Direct the groups to divide their stories into manageable segments.
- Have them condense and rewrite each segment so that it fits comfortably on one sheet. Make sure there is enough room for illustrations.
- Copy the text onto the acetate and illustrate each page.
- Store the transparencies in a self-sealing plastic bag.

Suggested Uses: Present research reports using this format. Creative stories and poems can be written on transparencies. Use them to illustrate rare Egyptian letters or numerals.

Ancient Wonders

The ancient Egyptian pyramids are one of the Seven Wonders of the Ancient World. Use an encyclopedia or other reference book to help you fill in the missing information about these magnificent structures. (On Your Own: Draw a map of the ancient world, locating each of the ancient wonders.)

Name	Location	When Built	Description
			Tombs built for Egyptian kings
	Babylon	between 605 and 562 B.C.	
			huge bronze statue of the god Apollo
Temple of Artemis		about 550 B.C.	
Lighthouse of Alexandria		between 283–246 B.C	
	Olympia, Greece		gold and ivory statue of Zeus
	Halicarnassus		huge white marble tomb

Internet Extender

Seven Wonders of the World Game

http://www.pbs.org/wgbh/nova/sunken/wonders/

Activity Summary: The notion of the Seven Wonders of the Ancient World can be traced back to the fifth century B.C. In their size, majesty, and beauty, these creations rivaled many created by nature. Today, the only remaining Wonder is the Great Pyramid. This game begins with unidentified pictures of the Seven Wonders of the World. Can you name them?" to find clues for the description, location (click on map), and history of #1. Return after you have read the clues and then click on the picture you think fits them. If you are wrong, return to the clues and try again. If you are successful, click on "continue" to identify the rest of the Wonders.

The Egypt Game

by Zilpha Keatley Snyder

Summary

The day April arrived at her grandmother's house she determined to live her life as she was used to. After all, it was only temporary, and her mother was sure to send for her soon. Grandma Caroline wisely tried to help April adjust by introducing her to a downstairs family, the Rosses. Their daughter Melanie quickly befriended April when they discovered a common interest—Egypt. Together they learned all they could about Egypt, its history, rituals, and people. When they stumbled on a deserted storage yard, the Egypt Game began in earnest. It started with three players, but a new girl at school was enlisted to join the group. Their costumes and ceremonies became more elaborate with each meeting. Then on Halloween night two boys from their class discovered the land of Egypt and they, too, became involved with the gang. Together the six boys and girls built an elaborate, imaginative world until strange, unexplainable things began to happen. In the exciting conclusion of the story, this mystery—along with the town's own murder mystery—is solved.

The outline below is a suggested plan for using the various activities that are presented in this unit. You should adapt these ideas to fit your own classroom situation.

Sample Plan

Day I

- Establish Elements of a Mystery (page 34).
- Mystery Words (page 34).
- Identifying Mystery Elements (page 34).
- Predict Story Events.
- Assign Chapters 1–5 (pages 3–49) in *The Egypt Game*.
- Begin the Chapter Activities (pages 37–38).

Day II

- Assign Chapters 6–10 (pages 50–97) in *The Egypt Game*.
- Continue the Chapter Activities (pages 38–39).
- Play Bingo (see Vocabulary Boosters, page 43).
- Critical Thinking: Relationships between words (see Side by Side, page 47).
- Math: Gods and Goddesses Galore (page 54).

Day III

- Assign Chapters 11–15 (pages 98–141) in *The Egypt Game*.
- Continue the Chapter Activities (pages 39–40).

- Alphabetizing Game (see Vocabulary Boosters, page 43).
- Write Story Frames (page 46).
- Social Studies: Research Nefertiti and Cleopatra Follow-up Quiz (page 58).
- Visit Web sites in the Internet Extender to learn more about Cleopatra (page 58).
- Math: Study triangles (page 64).

Day IV

- Assign Chapters 16–20 (pages 142–184) in *The Egypt Game*.
- Continue Chapter Activities (pages 40–41).
- Synonymous Crossword Puzzle (page 51); use with *The Egypt Game* Vocabulary (page 42).
- Art: Make 3-D mummies (page 55).
- Idioms: Figuratively Speaking (page 53).

Day V

- Assign Chapters 21–23 (pages 185–215) in *The Egypt Game*.
- Complete the Chapter Activities (page 41).
- Problems and Solutions (page 49).
- Sequencing Story Events (page 50).
- Identifying Characters (page 52).
- Making Books Ideas (page 56).

Overview of Activities

SETTING THE STAGE

1. **Prepare the class for a mystery:** Ask for a show of hands of those students who have done the following: read a Hardy Boys or Nancy Drew mystery; seen an episode of Murder She Wrote; seen an Alfred Hitchcock film. How could they tell it was a mystery? Establish some elements of a mystery. Record them on a chart and display it throughout the unit so it can be easily referred to.

Mystery Elements

1. Excitement
2. Clues
3. Crimes or Mystery
4. Detection
5. Suspense

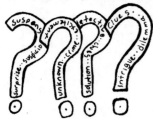

2. **Pair the students.** Direct each pair to make a large question mark out of tagboard or construction paper; cut it out. Give them fifteen minutes to write all the words they can think of that have to do with a mystery story. Share the lists in whole group before displaying the question marks on the wall.

3. **Watch a Sherlock Holmes film, an episode of *Unsolved Mysteries,* or read an Edgar Allan Poe story to the class.** Beforehand, group the students and assign each group to identify a specific mystery element in the plot. For example, group one should look for examples of the clues; group two should look for examples of suspense, etc.

4. **Prepare a Mystery Box by placing an object in a box.** Students can guess the contents from its weight, or they can shake the box. Provide one new clue each day until the mystery item is identified.

5. **Tell the class that they will be reading a mystery called *The Egypt Game.*** The setting is a large university town in California in the late 1960s. Predict possible story events based on the title; record the responses on chart paper. Roll it up and put it away. After the story has been completed take out the chart and compare it with the actual story events.

ENJOYING THE BOOK

1. **Schedule of Chapters**—See the Sample Plan on page 33 for suggested amounts. As students complete their assigned reading you may want to incorporate the Chapter Activities (see pages 37-41) into your lesson plans.

2. **Egypt Game Vocabulary**—Supply each student with a copy of the vocabulary page (page 42) as a number of assignments are correlated with it. Also, you may want to make an overhead transparency of this page (see #2 on page 73), or you could copy the words to make a giant wall chart.

3. **Vocabulary Boosters**—Page 43 is chock-full of vocabulary games for your students. In "Search and Find," pairs or groups can identify all words with prefixes or suffixes or both. Have them make a chart of their findings. Denote prefixes and suffixes with a highlighter pen.

Prefixes	Suffixes
reserved	priestess
upsweep	ducked
	warily

Overview of Activities *(cont.)*

ENJOYING THE BOOK *(cont.)*

---

4. **Guide words**—This exercise from page 43 will provide students with practice in alphabetizing and using guide words in a dictionary. An oral activity, it requires little advance preparation.

5. **Bingo**—Here is an old favorite with a new twist. Have the students make their own bingo cards, using the card on page 44. Choose one student to be the caller. Players count the number of syllables in the word called and place a marker on a word on their bingo card that has the same number of syllables. Keep playing until five or six students have a Bingo. See page 43 for complete directions.

6. **Alphabetizing**—This manipulative alphabetizing game (see page 43) is also a competition between groups. Students can make their own word strips, or you may use the words on page 45.

7. **Story Frames**—Practice sentence structure and continue to develop parts of speech with the outline provided on page 46. Follow-up activities are also provided.

8. **Write It**—On page 47 you will find five different writing assignments to develop critical thinking skills as well as writing skills. Sample forms for the Side by Side and the What's So Mysterious? activities are provided on page 48. All of the projects described are great partner activities.

9. **No Problem**—Present a math problem to the class. How many solutions can they find? Establish that the characters in *The Egypt Game* faced a number of problems but that a solution was always found. Students can practice writing solutions on page 49.

10. **Events in Sequence**—After the book has been read, recall story events with the class. Sequence the events. For further practice, use the events listed on page 50. Tell the students to sequence each group of events. Challenge them to write all twenty-four story events in correct story order.

11. **Synonymous Crossword Puzzle**—The crossword puzzle on page 51 will provide a challenge for even the most talented students. Remind them to use synonyms of the clues given. Students may want to work in pairs to complete this puzzle. Encourage the use of a thesaurus.

12. **Descriptions**—Tell the students to find a description of a character anywhere in the text. Call on a student to read the description without mentioning the character's name. Have the others in the class guess the name of the character. Follow up this activity with the worksheet on page 52.

13. **Figuratively Speaking**—Idioms abound in *The Egypt Game*. Direct the students to find idioms in the text, and/or find the idioms and explain them on page 53.

Overview of Activities *(cont.)*

ENJOYING THE BOOK *(cont.)*

14. **Gods and Goddesses Galore**—The Egypt game members learned about many Egyptian gods during the course of their activities. Find out the names of some other gods and goddesses and practice reducing fractions to their lowest terms at the same time (see page 54.)

15. **Be Crafty**—Page 55 contains two very clever craft ideas for making papyrus scrolls and a three-dimensional mummy. Both will be fun for the students to make.

EXTENDING THE BOOK

1. **Culminating Books**—An excellent way to wrap up a unit is to write a book. Two different options are presented on page 56. The multi-flap book requires patience and more time to complete than the flap book, but the results are well worth the extra effort. Writing topics for each type of book are also provided.

2. **Follow-Ups**—This page (57) is a gold mine of follow-up activities to do after the book has been completed. Art projects, suggested further reading, a construction project, and more are outlined here. Divide students into eight groups and assign each one a different project or allow them to choose their own.

3. **Nefertiti and Cleopatra**—Have the students research Queen Nefertiti and Cleopatra. Let them test their knowledge with the quiz at the top of page 58. Have the students investigate more about the fascinating, legendary Cleopatra by visiting the Web sites described in the Internet Extenders on page 58.

4. **Meet the Author**—Zilpha Keatley Snyder is the author of many outstanding books for children, including *The Egypt Game*, *The Headless Cupid*, and *The Witches of Worm*. Encourage the students to read some of her other titles. Discuss what makes her books so appealing.

5. **Sequel**—At the conclusion of *The Egypt Game*, April asks Melanie what she knows about gypsies, leading the reader to believe that the children's next adventures will be about gypsies. Have students write a sequel to *The Egypt Game*, using transparencies (see page 31). Groups can present their transparency stories to the whole class.

6. **Discussion**—As a group, discuss how April changed during the course of the story. Construct a chart to compare April's personality and behavior when she first arrived at Casa Rosada to her demeanor after the Egypt game was played out.

Chapter Activities

If you assign a specified number of pages or chapters each day, the ideas and activities presented below will be particularly helpful for reinforcing the text. Of course, these plans may also be implemented upon the completion of the entire book. Choose those activities that are best suited for your class. For your purposes, brief answers have been supplied in parentheses where applicable.

The Discovery of Egypt

For Discussion: What is the setting of the story? (*Large university town in California not long ago.*) The neighborhood was comprised of people of various cultures, but they all had something in common. What was it? (*A vague, mysterious fear of an old man called the Professor.*) How did the Professor stumble on *The Egypt Game*? (*Slight noise drew him to a window when he was in a seldom-used storeroom.*)

Activities: Based on the description given, draw a picture of the Professor. Find pictures of a thistle blossom and a lotus blossom; compare the two in a chart or poster.

Enter April

For Discussion: Why did April come to Casa Rosada? (*She'd been sent by her mother to live with her grandmother.*) Why did April call her grandmother Caroline? (*To be like her mother Dorothea; also, Caroline wasn't Dorothea's mother.*) Do you think Petrified Birthday Cake is a good name for Casa Rosada? Why or why not? (*Answers may vary.*)

Activities: Translate "Casa Rosada" to English. Find out what is meant by reincarnation. Draw and color a picture of Casa Rosada.

Enter Melanie and Marshall

For Discussion: Why was Melanie eagerly awaiting April's arrival? (*To have a friend handy.*) What was April's purpose in dressing as she did to meet Melanie? (*To make a definite impression.*) Describe the paper-families game. (*Made-up families; cut out pictures of them from magazines and catalogs; make up their personalities and what they do.*)

Activities: Invent a paper family: Cut out pictures from magazines; describe each family member. Write a story about an adventure that a paper family might have—use a cartoon format.

The Egypt Girls

For Discussion: Tell how the girls first became interested in Egypt (*April found a fascinating library book about Egypt.*) Why was April worried about the beginning of school? (*From experience, she knew it wasn't easy to face a new class.*) Why was Melanie worried about school starting? (*She feared that the other kids wouldn't put up with April's Hollywood act.*)

Activities: Write about a time when you were fearful; tell how you overcame your fearful feelings. Pretend your best friend shows you an outrageous outfit that he/she plans to wear to school. You know that others will ridicule your friend. Write a conversation you might have with your companion to tactfully let him/her know the outfit will be the object of ridicule.

Chapter Activities *(cont.)*

The Evil God and the Secret Spy

For Discussion: Predict what the Professor might do if he caught the children in the yard. (*Answers may vary.*) What do the girls think the Professor will do? (*Nothing—don't think he'd care.*) Why was Marshall reluctant to play the girl's game? (*He thought they might hurt him.*) What Egyptian name did they give Marshall? (*Marshamosis.*)

Activities: Draw a wanted poster of an evil god; describe him, his evil deeds, where he was last seen, the reward, etc. Recreate the altar from the story by building a miniature altar out of empty food containers, boxes, etc.

Eyelashes and Ceremony

For Discussion: What was occupying April's thoughts? (*Going home to Dorothea.*) What did Melanie do with April's eyelashes? (*Took them home and hid them.*) What nickname did Toby and Ken give April? (*February*) What did the girls use to record their rituals? (*Onion skin paper rolled on pieces of fishing pole.*) What was the Crocodile Stone? (*A stone Melanie found on the sidewalk; it resembled a crocodile snout.*)

Activities: Find a stone that resembles an animal; name it and see if your classmates agree with your name. Fold a sheet of paper in half. Write "pro" at the top of one side and "con" at the top of the other. Write reasons in each section for and against Melanie's hiding of April's eyelashes.

Neferbeth

For Discussion: Why is April reluctant to allow Elizabeth into their Egypt game? (*She thinks Elizabeth will tell others about their secret.*) What changed April's attitude toward Elizabeth? (*She thought she looked like Nefertiti.*)

Activities: Find and read the poem that begins, "April is the cruelest month" (From "The Burial of the Dead" in T.S. Eliot's *The Waste Land*). Draw a profile of someone in the class without lifting up your pencil and without glancing at your paper.

Prisoners of Fear

For Discussion: Predict what you think the "trouble in the neighborhood" could be. (*Answers may vary.*) Everyone had theories about the murder; which one do you believe? (*Answers may vary.*) Why did *The Egypt Game* maintain the Professor's innocence? (*April said it was a feeling she had.*) How did the four Egyptians cope without *The Egypt Game* to occupy them? (*They started to make costumes.*)

Activities: Write your own "Hymn to Isis." Create an Egyptian crown or headdress using a bleach bottle or some other materials. Read "Isis and Osiris" from *The First Book of Ancient Egypt* by Charles Moz.

Summoned by the Mighty Ones

For Discussion: How did April defend her plan to visit Egypt? (*No one had forbidden them to visit Egypt on Halloween night.*) Why might a trip to Egypt be "deadly dangerous?" (*Even if the Professor was innocent someone else in the neighborhood might be the murderer.*) How was April's relationship with her grandmother improving? (*She let Caroline help her with her hair and face; she smiled at her grandmother.*)

Activities: April had a pincushion box for special things. Find a small box and list all the things you can think of that are tiny enough to fit in the box (e.g., a penny, a ring, a pair of false eyelashes, etc.). Melanie repeated the phrases "downright disobedient" and "deadly dangerous" in her mind. Make a list of ten more alliterative phrases beginning with **d.**

Chapter Activities (cont.)

The Return to Egypt

For Discussion: Why did April panic when Marshall asked for a sign? (*She thought he was playing The Egypt Game.*) Why didn't the girls want to laugh at Toby's jokes? (*They didn't want to encourage him.*) How do you know their costumes were a "success?" (*Everyone admired and asked about them.*) What did the shooting star signify? (*A secret omen.*)

Activities: Work with a partner to create a Halloween costume out of a cardboard box. Write a list of ten things people might have said when they saw the four Egyptians out trick-or-treating.

Egypt Invaded

For Discussion: Before reading this chapter predict some story events. Why was Elizabeth so pleased with herself? (*The girls liked her idea of writing a letter in blood.*) How did Marshall react when the Crocodile god said they must sacrifice Security? (*Shouted "No"; jumped up and down.*) What did they sacrifice? (*Chewed-off fingernails.*)

Activities: Do the Egypt walk. Make up a game similar to Simon Says; use Egyptian movements and name it Isis Says (or other appropriate title).

Elizabethan Diplomacy

For Discussion: How did the four Egyptians react when they discovered the invaders' identities? (*Angry and relieved.*) Elizabeth had a plan to gain the boys' sympathy so they wouldn't fink; do you think it was a good one? What would you have done? (*Answers may vary.*) Toby's costume wouldn't fit through the hole in the fence. What were some other alternatives he had? (*Take it off; find another way to climb back over the fence; flatten the boxes.*)

Activities: You are Toby and you decide to remove your costume. Write a conversation you might have with your dad when you arrive home carrying your costume. Draw a before and after picture of Toby in his costume.

Moods and Maybes

For Discussion: Do you think Toby's dad was fair to restrict him for three days? What punishment, if any, would you have given Toby? (*Answers may vary.*) How did Dorothea's letter affect April? (*She tore it up in anger; cried.*) What did the boys think about the Egypt Game? (*Ken thought it was kooky; Toby wanted to hang around.*)

Activities: April didn't finish reading her mother's letter; complete it for her. How do you act when you're in a bad mood? Tell some things that help you get out of a bad mood.

Hieroglyphics

For Discussion: Name the Egyptian gods mentioned in this chapter. (*Isis, Bastet, Thoth.*) Why was April resistant to Toby's ideas (*It was her Egypt game.*) What is the story line of Aida? (*Tragic story of a beautiful princess who had been held captive in ancient Egypt.*) How did the Egypt gang raise money to buy colored pens? (*Boys mowed lawns; girls found empty bottles to return to the grocery store.*) Do you think the hieroglyphics ideas was a good one? Why or why not? (*Answers may vary.*)

Activities: Listen to a recording of Aida; draw a picture after you've listened to one or two selections. Make a list of other ways to earn money besides mowing lawns and returning bottles. Read the book *Aida* by Leontyne Price (HBJ, 1990).

Chapter Activities *(cont.)*

The Ceremony for the Dead

For Discussion: How did the girls explain Petey's death? (*He was Prince Pete-ho-top, son of Neferbeth Y and had fallen in battle.*) How did their Ceremony of the Dead develop? (*Stopped and started after discussions and new suggestions.*) Tell how the gang mummified Petey (*Soaked him in brine; anointed with spices and perfume wrapped in oil-soaked cloth.*)

Activities: Read *Mummies Made in Egypt* by Aliki (Harper Trophy, 1979). Compare the Egyptian process of mummification with the ceremonies the Egypt Game followed.

The Oracle of Thoth

For Discussion: Explain how Mrs. Granger was responsible for the next phase of the Egypt Game. (*She mentioned oracles and Toby asked her to explain it.*) Whose idea about writing to the oracle was better—Toby's or April's? Why? (*Answers may vary.*) Explain this idiom: going off your rockers. (*Losing it; going crazy, etc.*)

Activities: Find out what an ibis is; compare it to an owl. If you could ask an oracle one question about the future what would you ask it?

The Oracle Speaks

For Discussion: How do you think the oracle answered Ken's question? (*Answers may vary.*) Who do you think wrote the answers? (*Answers may vary.*) What question do you think April will ask Thoth? (*Answers may vary.*)

Activities: Burn incense; tell how incense might contribute to the mood of a ceremony. Make up a wailing chant to begin a ceremony; perform it for the class.

Where Is Security?

For Discussion: Why do you think Security is an appropriate name for Marshall's octopus? (*He carries it everywhere; it's his "security blanket"*) Explain Thoth's answer to April's question (*Answers may vary.*) How did Toby convince the gang to continue the game? (*Called them chicken; said it was ok if everyone wanted to split.*)

Activities: Draw a picture or write a description of something you have carried as security. Research the octopus; find out about its habitat, what it eats, its protection system, etc.

Confession and Confusion

For Discussion: Predict why you think Toby was the most worried of all. (*Answers may vary.*) Who wrote the answer to Marshall's question? (*They didn't know, but Marshall thought Set did it.*) What was Ken's reaction to the missing Set and the finding of Security? (*He wanted to resign from the Egypt Game.*)

Activities: Ken says "Sheesh" whenever he's disgusted, embarrassed, or upset; write some acceptable words you could say when you feel disgusted, etc. Read a book of quotations; find one about friends that would aptly describe the Egypt gang.

Fear Strikes

For Discussion: Why do you think the Egyptians didn't play games or consult the oracle anymore? (*They were afraid, confused, unsure.*) Was April a good babysitter? Explain your answer. (*Answers may vary.*) How did Marshall convince April to let him come to Egypt with her? (*He threatened to yell.*)

Chapter Activities *(cont.)*

Fear Strikes *(cont.)*

How was April freed from the stranglehold? (*Someone yelled for help and the attacker fled.*) Whose voice kept calling for help? (*Answers may vary.*)

Activities: Make a list of activities to use when babysitting. Play a game of Mousetrap. Marshall was doing something with a box and two orange juice cans; tell something you could make out of these materials.

The Hero

For Discussion: April was physically shaken by the experience; what would your reaction be in a similar situation? (*Answers may vary.*) What did the inspector mean when he said Marshall was looking as cool as a cucumber? (*He was acting calmly.*) How did Marshall describe April's attacker? (*Spotted man with orange hair.*) Why was Marshall a hero to the neighborhood? (*He'd identified Mr. Schmitt's cousin as the culprit.*)

Activities: Draw a picture of a spotted man with orange hair. Write a newspaper article telling about the incident and the subsequent apprehension of the criminal.

Gains and Losses

For Discussion: Explain what Egypt had meant to its six members (*Exciting, mysterious, imaginative, a private hideaway from grownups, shared with best friends.*) How had the Professor's store changed? (*Cleaner, brighter, not so cluttered; Mrs. Chung worked there.*) Were you pleased or surprised by April's answer to her mother's letter? How would you have replied? (*Answers may vary.*)

Activities: Make a greeting card for April to give to the Professor to thank him for saving her life. What is alabaster, what are some of its uses, and where is it found?

Christmas Keys

For Discussion: What did the Professor's Christmas story really reveal? (*That he was human.*) Why did the Professor begin watching the Egypt Game? (*To make sure nothing was damaged and no fires were started.*) Do you think the Professor's gifts to the children were appropriate? Why? (*Answers may vary.*) What gift did the children give the Professor? (*Answers may vary.*) Do you think they'll return to Egypt? Why? (*Answers may vary.*)

Activities: Outline some events that might occur in your sequel—*The Gypsy Game*. Write one chapter of *The Gypsy Game*.

Afterward

- Before each chapter, predict what might happen based on its title, or after each chapter predict what will happen next.
- Describe how April's relationship with her grandmother changes over the course of this story.
- Explain how April's relationship with her mother changes during the story.
- Compare any two characters in a Venn diagram.
- Choose a favorite character. Tell why he/she is your favorite.
- On a scale of one to ten, one being worst and ten being best, rate this book.

The Egypt Game Vocabulary

See suggested uses on page 43.

People, Places, and Things

curios	ritual	innovation	facade	vocalist	alley
escapades	caper	deadlock	pilgrimage	tomb	Horemheb
monoliths	mystic	prostrations	crinoline	snout	procession
chant	fink	populace	impression	soul	Nefertiti
Aida	resemblance	medley	theories	petitions	splendors
consensus	scheme	tendency	assurance	alabaster	alibi
oracle	Security	Anubis	Thoth	Set	Bastet
Neferbeth	Marshamosis	Egyptologist	anthropology	consternation	rebellion
Ramos	reincarnation	Casa Rosada	hi-fi	upsweep	omen
momentum	leads	convulsions	inspiration	grottoes	seclusion
hieroglyphs	incense	priestess	ceremony	lair	brine
bier	Egypt	drone	oracle	version	demonstrations
		oath	pharaoh		

Descriptive Words

vague	dingy	improbable	pert	sturdily	plush
taut	frantic	fascinating	fragrant	primitive	corrugated
sinister	predictable	balefully	supernatural	steadfastly	jet-propelled
righteous	sacrificial	defiantly	exasperated	raptly	fluent
reassuring	gravelly	sympathetic	pale	haughty	soberly
scornfully	sturdy	gingerly	regal	extravagant	prim
dead-pan	drastic	treacherous	persistent	haughtily	indelicately
incredulous	intent	ornate	exotic	evasive	mystic
drone	fiendish	exalted	hazy	petrified	warily

Action Words

torment	postponed	ad-libbed	coaxed	mugged	meditated
slither	scurried	leer	milling	fuming	flick
perched	presided	prompted	ambushed	teetered	curled
swagger	faltered	peered	flourish	reserved	rasped
accumulated	languishing	wilt	console	deciphered	bounded
surrounded	ducked	integrate	clamored	quavered	contemplated
dispense	consult	blabbed	eliminating	glared	lingering
parroted	sidled	spouted	gloat	stacked	conceived

42

Vocabulary Boosters

Below are some easy games and activities to boost and expand vocabulary skills. Sample lists of vocabulary words can be found on page 42.

Search and Find

Pair or group the students. Provide each group with a vocabulary list (page 42). Direct them to find and write a list of all the words that contain a prefix; a suffix; or both. Circle or highlight the prefixes and suffixes.

Guide Words

Make an overhead transparency of page 42 (for how-to's see page 73) and display. Or, supply each student or group with a copy of page 42. On the chalkboard write any two words to act as guides. Then have students identify a word from the list that would appear between these two guide words. For example, write *insight* and *invest* on the board. Correct responses would include intent, inspiration, integrate. At your discretion students may quietly stand or raise their hands when they've found a word. Once students are familiar with the process, let them take turns giving guide words.

Bingo

Have the students make their own bingo cards, using specified words from the vocabulary list and the blank bingo card on page 44. Give each student a handful of markers (beans, coins, dry cereal, etc.). Make a calling card list of words. Cut each out, place in a bag or box and read them one at a time. The leader calls out a word from the calling card list. The student determines the number of syllables in the called-out word and places a marker on one word on his game card that has that same number of syllables. (For example, if "primitive" was called out, a student could place a marker on any three-syllable word on his/her game card.) Continue in this manner until a player has bingo (five in a row).

Alphabetizing

Write a different vocabulary word on each of several strips of paper. Make an exact set for each group of students. Or, use any of the three sample game cards on page 45. Give a set of vocabulary strips to each group. On a given signal, tell them to alphabetize the words. When their group has completed the task, they may quietly stand up. (This last step is optional but motivational!)

Partner Sentences

Pair the students. Display the vocabulary word list on the overhead projector (if you've made an overhead transparency) or supply each pair with a copy of the words. One partner chooses a word from each category and tells them to his/her partner who must then write a sentence using all three words. Have the partners exchange roles. Tell them to write four sentences each. Variation: Choose all three words from one category only.

Bingo Card

Make enough copies for each student to have one card. For complete playing directions, see page 43.

		FREE SPACE		

Alphabetizing Game Cards

Make a copy of the same set of game cards for each group to alphabetize. Cut the cards apart on the solid lines before giving them to the students. Game directions are on page 43.

resemblance	righteous
momentum	procession
scheme	torment
teetered	spouted
soberly	reserved

bier	Bastet
faltered	brine
balefully	flick
bounded	fluent
flourish	frantic

assurance	Anubis
accumulated	alabaster
alibi	anthropology
ambushed	ad-libbed

Name _____

Story Frame

Work with a group to complete each of the sentences below. Use words from the vocabulary list on page 42.

1. In a very short time they had _____all sorts of
   _____ facts about_____ and temples,
   _____ and _____ , mummies and
   _____ , and dozens of other _____ topics.

2. They_____down two blocks without seeing a _____ ,
   turned the corner, and a moment later _____into the
   _____that led to_____ .

3. Her hair was _____ up in a pile that seemed to be more
   pins than hair, and the whole thing_____
   forward over her thin _____ face.

4. The huge _____owl seemed to be leaning forward, staring into the _____
   burner; and as they watched, a final twist of _____smoke _____
   upward like a dancing snake....

5. At the next_____ , which was to be the presentation of a dead lizard
   as a _____ offering to Set,
   Marshall marched at the head of the _____ .

More Activities

Choose and complete one or more of the following projects.

1. Rewrite the sentences above, using words of your own choice.

2. Choose one sentence from the five above. Rewrite it as many different ways as you can, using words from the vocabulary list on page 42.

3. Illustrate each sentence. Cut out each sentence, glue it to the bottom of a sheet of paper, and draw a picture in the space.

Write It

Develop critical thinking skills, vocabulary, and writing skills with the following assignments. Choose those activities which are appropriate for your students.

Side by Side

- Choose a theme—the Nile River, for example.

- Brainstorm some things that are related to the Nile and that also go together—cataract and delta, for example.

- Write the word pairs in a format similar to the example on the right (or use the sample form on page 48).

- Tell students to be prepared to explain the relationship in each word pair.

> **Theme:** The Nile River
> These Things Are Related
>
> *cataract* and *delta*
> *hieroglyphics* and *papyrus*
> *crocodiles* and *Sobek*
> *pyramids* and *stones*
> _____ and _____

What's So Mysterious?

- With the students, brainstorm words related to *mystery*.

- Record these words and phrases on a "map" or outline. (You may use the sample form on page 48.)

- Add as many lines as needed.

Story Maps

- Have the students identify the the elements of a story plot—the characters, conflict, climax, and resolution.

- Divide the students into small groups and direct the groups to draw a picture of each element listed above. Label each one.

- Tell them to write a few sentences about each picture.

- Share with the whole group before displaying the work on the walls.

Point of View

- Establish that point of view refers to the angle from which a story is told. Point of view can be first person, where one character narrates the story (I chose Elizabeth to play the part of Queen Neferbeth), or third-person, where someone on the outside is telling the story (April chose Elizabeth to play the part of Queen Neferbeth).

- Have the students determine the point of view of *The Egypt Game*.

- Tell them to choose two paragraphs from the book and rewrite them using a different point of view.

More Elements

- Identify the protagonist, setting, theme, and tone of *The Egypt Game* in a whole-group discussion.

- Direct the students to write questions and a complete-sentence answer for each one. For example, Who is the protagonist of *The Egypt Game*? The protagonist of *The Egypt Game* is April Dawn Hall.

Forms for Write It

These two outlines are provided for use with the "Side by Side" and "What's So Mysterious?" writing projects described on page 47. Change and adapt the themes for different lesson topics.

Theme: _____

These Things Are Related

_____ and _____

_____ and _____

_____ and _____

_____ and _____

_____ and _____

_____ and _____

No Problem

Throughout *The Egypt Game* the characters are confronted with a number of problems, but a solution always seems to be found. One problem that arises early on, for example, is April's Hollywood act, and its effect on her classmates. Melanie solves the problem by acting as a go-between for the other sixth graders and April. The result is that things begin to get better, and the students regard April as... "their own private odd-ball."

Read each problem below and explain how each was resolved. Write your own problem and solution for number 8.

1. Problem: April plans to wear her false eyelashes to school.

   Solution: _____

   _____

2. Problem: Toby and Ken find out about the Egypt Game.

   Solution: _____

   _____

3. Problem: The boxes they gather to build an altar won't fit through the hole in the fence.

   Solution: _____

   _____

4. Problem: Marshall protests that he doesn't want to be the sacrifice in their game.

   Solution: _____

   _____

5. Problem: After the young girl's murder, no one is allowed to play outside.

   Solution: _____

   _____

6. Problem: Caroline suggests that the girls should ask the new girl, Elizabeth, to play.

   Solution: _____

   _____

7. Problem: Toby has not written the answer to Marshall's question to the oracle.

   Solution: _____

   _____

8. Problem: _____

   Solution: _____

   _____

Events in Sequence

Test your knowledge of the story events by sequencing the three events in each section: write a 1 next to the event that happened first, a 2 by the event that occurred next, and a 3 by the event that occurred last. For a real challenge, arrange all the story events below in chronological order; use the back of this paper. You may want to choose a partner for this activity.

_____ Following a discussion about oracles, Ken was chosen to write the first question. _____ Toby brought a stuffed owl to Egypt, and they named it Thoth. _____ Much to their amazement, Ken's question had been answered by Thoth.		**1**
_____ Mrs. Ross abruptly interrupted their Egypt game. _____ When the girls met Elizabeth, they were surprised by her tiny stature. _____ A bleach bottle and a plastic bowling pin became a pharaoh's crown for Marshall.		**2**
_____ The Professor gave each of the children a key to Egypt. _____ Mr. Schmitt's stockboy was apprehended and charged with the crimes. _____ Someone yelled for help as April was being strangled.		**3**
_____ The girls begged Toby and Ken not to fink on them. _____ Dorothea wrote April to tell her she'd married Nick. _____ Ken and Toby displayed genuine interest in the Egypt Game and wanted to join the gang.		**4**
_____ While babysitting Marshall, April realized she'd left her math book in Egypt. _____ After April's question was answered, Toby suggested they quit the oracle bit. _____ Toby confessed to being the oracle and writing answers to the questions.		**5**
_____ Melanie introduced April to her paper-families game. _____ Marshall was given the title Marshamosis, king of all the Egyptians. _____ They discovered Egypt in a weed-filled, deserted yard.		**6**
_____ Petey, Elizabeth's dead parakeet, was soaked in brine in preparation for burial. _____ Security was lost in Egypt. _____ The Egyptians spent their next few meetings learning the hieroglyphic alphabet.		**7**
_____ A huge misshapen figure sprang forward and landed right in the middle of Egypt. _____ Everyone made a fuss over Elizabeth and Marshall in their Egyptian costumes. _____ They planned to go trick-or-treating briefly before going to Egypt.		**8**

A Synonymous Crossword Puzzle

Complete this crossword puzzle in the same manner you always do. Just use synonyms for the clues that are given. Hint: All synonyms can be found in *The Egypt Game*.

Across

4. evil
6. showy
8. tattled
9. directed
10. gazed
13. escapade
15. aromatic
18. cautiously
19. disbelieving
21. phonograph
24. murky
25. mimicked
26. droop
27. smirk

Down

1. intently
2. nudged
3. colorless
4. plan
5. brainstorm
7. kingly
11. rite
12. monotone
13. knicknacks
14. severe
16. trapped
17. strong
19. engrossed
20. grimy
22. indefinite
23. spirit
25. proper

On Your Own

- Use vocabulary words from *The Egypt Game* to make an antonym crossword puzzle.
- Find antonyms for other words from the vocabulary list on page 42.

Name _____

Descriptions

Identify the characters by reading the descriptive phrases. Write the proper name in the space provided. Use the Character Name Box to help you.

Character Name Box

Security	Toby	Ken	Melanie	Casa Rosada
Elizabeth	Marshall	Caroline	Mr. Bodler	Dorothea
April	Mrs. Ross	Professor	Mr. Ross	Mr. Schmitt's cousin

1. _____ "...tall and bent and his thin beard straggled up his cheeks..."

2. _____ "...Spanishy-looking with great thick walls, arched doorways..."

3. _____ "...looked sharp and neat with a smart-looking very short hairdo..."

4. _____ "...a stocky red-headed young man with blotchy freckles..."

5. _____ "...amazingly tiny for a fourth grader..."

6. _____ "...thin and palely blond...hair arranged in a straggly pile""

7. _____ "...sort of cute in a big blunt cocky way."

8. _____ "...was black...pert features and slender-arching eyebrows..."

9. _____ "...wore her gray hair in a bun on the back of her head."

10. _____ "...had a special talent for getting people off the hook..."

11. _____ "...pear-shaped plush body and six of his black legs were hanging..."

12. _____ "...His funny little baby-round chin was sticking out defiantly..."

13. _____ "...she's a singer and in the movies, and stuff like that."

14. _____ "...a fattish man with faded blond hair...noisily cheerful at children..."

15. _____ "...He was sitting on the couch surrounded by books and paper."

52

Name _____

Figuratively Speaking

Throughout *The Egypt Game* the author employs idioms to make the text more interesting. Idioms are figures of speech or expressions that say one thing but mean something different. For example, when people say "It is raining cats and dogs," they actually mean that it is pouring heavily. Read each line below. Underline the idioms and explain them on the lines provided.

1. "But by Friday April was in a much better frame of mind." _____
_____

2. "Toby Alvillar and Ken Kamata were two of the biggest wheels in class...." _____
_____

3. "Sometimes I think the whole bunch of you guys are going off your rockers." _____
_____

4. "...every kid would feel duty bound to do his part in trimming the new kid down to size." _____
_____

5. "...Toby had a special talent for getting people off the hook by making the teacher laugh." _____
_____

6. "You really are cracking up this time." _____
_____

7. "...Mr. Ross had to study and he was only too glad for the girls to get Marshall out from underfoot." _____
_____

8. "He'd picked on a subject that Mrs. Granger could really get her teeth into." _____
_____

9. "...if you're so crazy about excitement why don't you go jump off the bridge or something?" ____
_____

10. "I think you guys are a bunch of chickens." _____
_____

11. "Just when things get good and something really exciting starts happening, you want to cop out."_
_____
_____

12. "Then if you don't dig it," he shrugged, "we won't do it." _____
_____

The Egypt Game

Name _____

Gods and Goddesses Galore

Ancient Egyptians worshiped over one hundred gods and goddesses. There were gods and goddesses for every occasion, including childbirth, snake bites, illness, and death. Some gods and goddesses took on the forms of animals, while others had human characteristics.

Find out the names of some of these gods and goddesses by reducing each fraction to its lowest terms. Look for its equivalent in the fraction box below. Write the letter from the box on the proper space. Word clues and some letters are given to help you.

Fraction	¼ **M**	⅓ **T**	1/20 **G**	⅙ **K**	⅐ **W**	⅑ **N**
Box	1/12 **R**	⅛ **S**	½ **B**	1/10 **H**	1/11 **P**	⅕ **Y**

---

1. a fat dwarf with the ears and mane of a lion; the protector of newborns

   ___ ___(e)___ ___ ___
   $\frac{4}{8}$ $\frac{5}{40}$

5. the vulture goddess

   ___(e)___ ___ ___ ___(e)___ ___
   $\frac{3}{27}$ $\frac{2}{12}$ $\frac{5}{50}$ $\frac{17}{34}$ $\frac{2}{6}$

---

2. a ram-headed god who presided over the hazardous cataracts (rapids) of the Nile

   ___ ___(u)___(e)___ ___
   $\frac{3}{18}$ $\frac{4}{40}$ $\frac{2}{18}$ $\frac{12}{48}$ $\frac{7}{42}$

6. the creator god symbolized by a scarab beetle

   ___ ___ ___
   $\frac{2}{20}$ $\frac{3}{33}$ $\frac{5}{60}$

---

3. the crocodile god

   ___(o)___ ___(e)___
   $\frac{3}{24}$ $\frac{25}{50}$ $\frac{4}{24}$

7. goddess of war; she had the head of a lion

   ___(e)___ ___ ___ ___(e)___ ___
   $\frac{4}{32}$ $\frac{6}{36}$ $\frac{7}{70}$ $\frac{4}{16}$ $\frac{8}{24}$

---

4. goddess who protected pregnant women from evil creatures

   ___(a)___ ___(e)___ ___(e)___
   $\frac{5}{45}$ $\frac{2}{14}$ $\frac{3}{36}$ $\frac{7}{21}$

8. cobra goddess; workmen prayed to her if they were bitten or stung

   ___(e)___ ___(e)___ ___(e)___ ___(e)___
   $\frac{3}{12}$ $\frac{2}{24}$ $\frac{9}{27}$ $\frac{2}{16}$ $\frac{4}{20}$ $\frac{4}{48}$

Be Crafty

April and Melanie were very creative with their costumes and the objects they used to create the Temple for the Egypt Game. Here are some other Egyptian crafts that you might like to try.

Papyrus Scrolls

Materials: onion paper (or other parchment paper; available in stationery stores); clear tape; cardboard tubes (cut from foil or wax paper rolls)

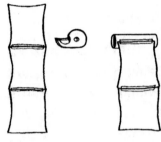

Directions:

- Place several sheets of the paper together end to end.
- Tape all the way across where two pages meet, both front and back.
- When the sheets are taped together, tape the top sheet to the outside of the cardboard roll.
- Tape the bottom sheet to the other roll and curl the two rolls towards one another like a scroll.
- Use the scroll to write your own hieroglyphics or creative story.

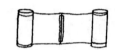

It's a Mummy

Materials: colored 8½" x 11" (22 cm x 28 cm) index stock or heavy paper; white typing paper; bold-line black marker; scissors; glue; colored pencils or markers; pencil

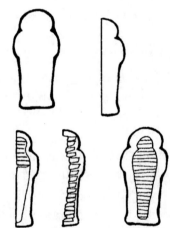

Directions:

- Draw a mummy pattern onto the white paper. Cut it out.
- Make a bold outline all along the edge of the pattern.
- Fold the paper pattern in half. With a pencil lightly draw an outline of the mummy.
- With the scissors, cut straight strips from the folded edge to the outline. (You may want to draw the lines with a ruler before cutting.)
- A few at a time, fold the strips back along the outline; unfold
- Turn the shape over; fold and unfold the strips.
- Carefully open up the paper.
- Hold the top and the bottom of the mummy; press the strips through to the other side.
- Fold the paper in half and press the strips flat. Open up.
- Glue the mummy to the center of the index stock.
- With the marking pen, draw a sarcophagus around the shape.
- Draw hieroglyphics on the sarcophagus.
- Color the background brown to make it look dark inside the tomb.

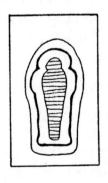

Culminating Books

As a culminating project for *The Egypt Game,* direct the students to make a book. Present them with both options below, and let them choose one to complete or assign each pair or group a specific idea.

Flap Book

Materials: Pencil; wide marking pen; construction paper or tagboard; writing paper; stapler

Directions:

- Have the students draw an Egyptian shape—a hippo, the outline of the Sphinx, Nefertiti's head, etc., or use the mummy pattern on page 72.
- For more stability, glue the shape to construction paper, tagboard, or other heavy paper; cut out around the outline.
- With the marking pen, draw a wide outline along the edge of the shape.
- Cut out paper rectangles or squares that will fit inside the shape. Use these for writing the story.
- When the writing has been completed, place the rectangles one on top of each other in correct story order. Staple to the body of the shape.
- Add details to the shape, if desired.

Writing Topics

- On each page write a different mysterious event from *The Egypt Game.*
- Draw a story map of the plot; include characters, conflict, climax, and resolution.
- Describe each character in detail. Include their physical appearances and personality traits.

Multi Flap Book

Materials: Oak tag or poster board; cardboard (a side cut from a box); skills knife or box cutter; glue; finetip marking pens; pencil; ruler.

Directions:

- Fold a sheet of oaktag or poster board in half.
- Draw a shape outline; draw one edge on the fold.
- Keep folded and cut out; lay it flat on the cardboard on a flat surface.
- With a pencil and ruler, lightly draw squares on the body of the shape that is on the right side.
- Cut along the bottom and two sides only of each square; fold up.
- Fold the shape together so the flaps are facing out and up.
- Glue the two shapes together. Do not glue the area behind the flaps.
- Use the marking pens to write on and underneath each flap; add details to the shape, if desired.

Wrting Topics:

- Write a question about a character on the flap; write the answer in the space behind the flap. For example. Who witnessed the Egypt Game from afar? the Professor
- On the top flap write a definition. Behind it, write the words.
- Write a word on the top flap and its antonym or synonym behind it.
- Use vocabulary from *The Egypt Game.*

Follow-Ups

Once students have completed reading *The Egypt Game,* follow it up with any of the activities on this page. For more effective projects, allow students to choose an activity which interests them.

- Read another mystery story. Choose from authors such as Mary Higgins Clark, Agatha Christie, Sir Arthur Conan Doyle, or Edgar Allan Poe.

- Convince others to read the book by reading a few paragraphs aloud to them—but don't give away the ending!

- Stamp a message with the Metropolitan Museum of Art's hieroglyphic stamp set and Fun with Hieroglyphics Stationery (the stationery includes colorful stickers). Both are available at book stores and teacher supply stores.

- Display a copy of Paul Klee's painting *Sinbad the Sailor.* It was inspired by a trip he made down the Nile River. Paint an Egyptian picture using squares. With colored pencils or markers, color the squares of 1-inch graph paper in various bright colors. Then draw a picture over the background using a black marker. Create a title for your artwork.

- Read *The Egyptian Cinderella* by Shirley Climo (Harper, 1989) or *The Prince Who Knew His Fate* by Lise Manniche (Putnam, 1982). Write your own Egyptian fairy tale based on what you know about ancient Egyptian beliefs.

- Build a giant pyramid from appliance boxes. Tape the edge together with duct tape or electrical tape. Cut an opening on one side for entry. Use it as a private reading room, "think tank," or creative writing center. For more complete directions, see *The Pyramids* by Harriette Abels (Crestwood House, 1987).

- Create a system of hieroglyphs. Write a short story on 3" x 5" (8 cm x 13 cm) index cards. Staple cards together at the left side. Now write the same story using your hieroglyph system. Staple those cards together. Attach both stories, one above the other, to a cardboard or tagboard background.

- Use a styrofoam head base (used to hold wigs; available in beauty supply stores) or make one out of papier mâché. Apply makeup to resemble Cleopatra or Nefertiti. Make a paper or yarn wig. Or, draw on oval on an 8½" x 11" (22 cm x 28 cm) sheet of white paper. With makeup, draw the features of an Egyptian princess.

- Play *Annabel's Dream of Ancient Egypt* an interactive video disc. It comes with reading materials, reference materials, and group activities; appropriate for grades 3–8. From Texas Canar; 3933 Spicewood Springs Road, Suite E-100, Austin, TX 78759.

Nefertiti and Cleopatra

In *The Egypt Game,* April and Melanie observe that Elizabeth bears a strong resemblance to Nefertiti, so she is given the role of Queen Neferbeth in their imaginative game. If Elizabeth had resembled Cleopatra, she might have been given the name Cleobeth.

Just who were Nefertiti and Cleopatra? Research both of these famous Egyptian women. Then read the sentences below. Circle **N** if the statement applies to Nefertiti. Circle **C** if the statement applies to Cleopatra.

1. N C   She was thought to be the mother-in-law of Tutankhamen.
2. N C   She was a descendant of the Ptolemies, a Greek family.
3. N C   She committed suicide by allowing herself to be bitten by an asp.
4. N C   Her brother exiled her so he could become the sole ruler of Egypt.
5. N C   The statue of her head is world-famous.
6. N C   She had one son.
7. N C   Her husband was the pharaoh Amenhotep IV.
8. N C   She had six daughters.
9. N C   She rolled herself up into a rug as a gift for Caesar.
10. N C   Mark Antony planned to make her his queen.
11. N C   Her husband changed his name to Akhenaten in honor of the sun god Aten.
12. N C   The Romans distrusted her.
13. N C   Her daughter Ankhesenamen was thought to be the wife of Tutankhamen.
14. N C   Her second child died in infancy.
15. N C   Caesar helped her regain the throne in Egypt.

Internet Extenders

Alexander the Great conquered Egypt's enemy, Persia, and was welcomed by them as a hero and made an Egyptian pharaoh. When Alexander died, one of his most powerful generals, Ptolemy, took over Egypt and was accepted by them as a part of Alexander's family. Ptolemy then became pharaoh—Ptolemy I. He set the name standard for the last of Egypt's great dynasties. All his male heirs were called Ptolemy, and his female successors were called Cleopatra. The last pharaoh was Cleopatra VII. Read more about this fascinating person at the Web sites below.

Cleopatra, the Last Pharaoh

http://www.interoz.com/egypt/cleopatr.htm

Activity Summary: This history of the last pharaoh of Egypt reads like a novel and is very detailed. It begins with Ptolemy's death in 51 B. C., which sets the wheels in motion for his daughter, Cleopatra VII, to carry on the dynasty.

What Did Cleopatra Wear?

http://www.xsite.net/~videoc/Cleo/Cleopatra1.html

Activity Summary: Learn what the last pharaoh, Cleopatra VII, most likely wore, including her makeup. Compare this with the costumes in the many films and stage productions about her.

Meet the Author

How many students would have guessed that Zilpha Keatly Snyder was once a public school teacher or that all six of the main characters in *The Egypt Game* were based on real children that she'd once taught? Uncover more interesting facts about Ms. Snyder and her career in the newspaper article below.

The Author's Gazette

WHO:	Zilpha Keatley Snyder was born May 11, 1927, in Lemoore, California. She married Larry Alan Snyder in 1950 and has one daughter and two sons. She graduated from Whittier College and also studied at the University of California, Berkeley.
WHAT:	Ms. Snyder began her career as a school teacher and taught upper grades for nine years in California, New York, Washington, and Alaska. She then switched to writing but credits her teaching experience as invaluable to her writing. As she explained, her students provided her with ideas, personalities, and language which she was able to incorporate into her writings.
WHERE:	Zilpha Keatley Snyder now lives with her husband in a northern California town close to San Francisco.
WHEN:	In 1964 *Season of Ponies* won an ALA Notable Book award.
	In 1965 *The Velvet Room* was named to be on the *Horn Book* honor list.
	In 1967 *The Egypt Game* received an ALA Notable Book award and was on the *Horn Book* honor list.
WHY:	Zilpha explains that she writes because she realized at an early age that writing is what she wanted to do. Her love of books grew out of the fact that during her childhood there wasn't much money—it was the Depression and World War II era. She turned to books and read nearly one a day throughout those early years.
HOW:	How can you find out more about Zilpha Keatley Snyder? Look in the reference section of the library for a series of books entitled *Something About the Author.*

To Do:

- Compose a letter to Ms. Snyder, telling her why you enjoyed *The Egypt Game*.
- Write an interview you would like to have with this author.

Ancient Egypt Vocabulary

This handy reference can be used in a number of ways: as a word bank for creative writing, rhymes, and poems; as a list of geography and social studies terms to know; and as a model for spelling and vocabulary development. Add to this list throughout the unit of studies.

Places

Memphis	Aswan	Red Sea	Mediterranean Sea	Upper Egypt	Red Land
Tura	Thebes	Nile River	Delta	Lower Egypt	Giza

Games and Toys

senet	clayballs
game of snake	spinning tops
paddle dolls	board games
khuzza lawizza (leapfrog)	tug-of-war
playing soldier	spinning dances
toy animals	playing catch

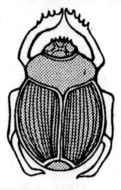

Famous People

King Tutankhamen
Ramses XI
King Khufu
Imhotep
King Djoser
King Sneferu
Queen Hetepheres
Hatshepsut
Queen Nefertiti
Akhenaten
Pepy II
Ramses the Great
Cleopatra

Gods and Goddesses

Osiris	Horus	Hapy	Udjat
Thoth	Imsety	Hathor	Isis
Anubis	Imsety	Hathor	Isis
Geb	Duamutef	Tefnut	Shu Re-horakhty
Nephthys	Sobek	Bastet	Ptah
Qebhsenuef			
Set			

Mummification

ba	ka
corpse	preserve
burial	embalm
mummy	natron
gods	goddesses
canopic	Jarnen
chemical	shrouds
binding	shabti
portrait mask	amulets
scarab	ankh
resin	cartonnage
coffin	sarcophagus
mourners	procession
"opening of the mouth"	

Other Terms

pharaoh	Sphinx
The Book of the Dead	papyrus
scrolls	everlasting
eternity	pyramid
tomb	hieroglyphs
monument	mastabas
temenos	mortuary
temple	immortal
porticullises	mortar
barge	courses
corridor	capstone
plumbline	incense
sanctuary	alabaster
capitals	anointed

Name _____

A Great Pyramid Puzzle

Review the words you have learned in your studies of ancient Egypt. You may want to work with a partner to complete this crossword puzzle.

Across

3. stone coffin in which wood coffin was placed

5. thin paper made from reeds

7. huge sculpted lion with a man's head

9. the fertile mouth of the Nile River

11. queen who helped her husband set up the cult of the sun god Aten

12. ancient capital of Egypt

14. the Great Pyramid at Giza was built for this ruler

15. name given to Egyptian kings

17. jars that held the embalmed organs

18. thirty-foot wall surrounding the base of the pyramid

19. the old capital of Egypt

Down

1. mixture of sand, lime, and water

2. Prince of the Dead

3. mummy-shaped amulet that held farm tools

4. translucent stone used in floor slabs

6. board game played with counters and throw sticks

7. an early board game in which players moved their counter around the squares

8. river which runs through Egypt

10. figures tucked in between the mummy's layers of wrappings

11. chemical used to preserve bodies

13. another word for mummify

16. Egyptian sign of life

The Animal Connection

To ancient Egyptians animals were the earthly versions of gods. For example, cats were sacred to the god Bastet, and crocodiles symbolized the god Sobek. Examples of animals permeate Egyptian artifacts and the system of hieroglyphs.

In modern society animals may not be regarded as gods, but the Egyptian influence can still be seen in our language. A number of our idioms compare human traits with animal traits. Who hasn't heard or used the expression, "I'm as hungry as a bear," for example? See how well you know your animal expressions by completing the following exercises.

I. Fill in each blank with the appropriate animal name.

1. as quiet as a(n) _____

2. as stubborn as a(n) _____

3. as sly as a(n) _____

4. as slippery as a(n) _____

5. as greedy as a(n) _____

6. as wise as a (n) _____

7. as gentle as a(n) _____

8. as clumsy as a(n) _____

9. as busy as a(n) _____

10. as tiny as a(n) _____

11. as big as a(n) _____

12. as happy as a(n) _____

II. In your own words explain each animal idiom below.

1. She eats like a bird. _____

2. Your goose is cooked. _____

3. Hold your horses. _____

4. He's like a bull in a china shop. _____

5. It's raining cats and dogs. _____

6. She's as mad as a wet hen. _____

7. Take the bull by the horns. _____

8. It's a one-horse town. _____

III. Invent your own expression for these animals.

1. goat _____

2. cow _____

3. hippopotamus _____

4. crocodile _____

Name _____

Picture Math

Try your hand at Egyptian math. Be sure to show all your work in Egyptian figures.

a. 𝟡∩∩||| × ∩∩∩|||||	**e.** ⟲∩∩||||| ∥ + 𝟛𝟛𝟛 𝟡𝟡∩|
b. Write 4,355 in Egyptian figures.	**f.** 𝟤 ÷ 𝟡𝟡∩∩|||||
c. 𝟤𝟤𝟡| − 𝟤∩∩∩∩∩ ∩	**g.** Write 1,000,220 in Egyptian figures.
d. 𝟡||| + 𝟡𝟡𝟡𝟡∩∩|||||| |||	**h.** 𝟡𝟡∩ ÷ |||||

Math Extensions

The study of pyramids leads easily and naturally to other math topics such as triangles, squares, and other solid figures. Some projects and ideas are outlined below to help you get started.

Triangles

- The sides of a regular pyramid are four congruent isosceles triangles. Have students find other examples of triangles in architecture. Tell them to cut out pictures from magazines and newspapers or bring in library books that contain applicable pictures.
- Challenge students to find out who Pythagoras was and what he contributed to the field of math. Present the Pythagorean Theorem ($a^2 + b^2 = c^2$) to the students.
- Construct angles and triangles with a compass.
- Measure the angles of various triangles with a protractor.
- Find out how artists used the Golden Triangle in their drawings (see Leonardo da Vinci).
- Learn the difference between congruent and similar triangles.
- Use a protractor to measure angles of common objects.

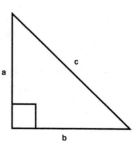

Squares

- The base of a pyramid was most often a square. Review what students know about squares (all sides are equal in length; all angles are right angles or 90°).

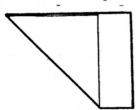

- Make paper squares. Take any size sheet of paper. Place it flat in front of you. Fold up the right corner to the left edge of the paper until a triangle is formed. Make a crease on the fold. Cut off the excess at the top of the paper and discard this piece. Open up the triangle. Measure it to see if it is really square.

- Look for examples of the use of squares in art. Examine works by Paul Klee. *The Niesen* contains a blue pyramid. Have the students draw or paint a picture using that style. For more information about Klee read *Paul Klee* by Ernest Raboff (Doubleday, 1968).

Solid Figures

- Display some solid figures—a tetrahedron, cube, octahedron, etc.
- Create solid figures using flour and salt dough (see recipe below) and cone-shaped paper cups, paper juice cans, and small rectangular paper boxes. Pack the dough into the containers. Carefully peel away the paper to reveal a solid figure.
- Construct a paper pyramid (see pattern on page 23).
- Challenge the students to create a pattern that will fold into a cube. There are a number of possible solutions—one example is at right—so allow various students to demonstrate theirs.
- **Dough Recipe:** In a bowl, mix together one cup (240 mL) each of flour, salt, and water. After mixing, knead the dough until it is smooth.

Animals of the Nile

Read the paragraph below. Find and circle the bold-faced animal names in the word search puzzle. Names may be up, down, across, or diagonal.

A wide variety of animals thrived in the deserts and flood plains of ancient Egypt. **Lions**, **wild bulls**, **antelopes**, and **gazelles** were plentiful in the desert east and west of the Nile Valley. **Hyenas**, **rams**, **jackals**, and **oxen** also inhabited those areas. **Birds** of all kinds made their home in the papyrus thickets beside the Nile. Nests of **pintail ducks**, **pelicans**, **geese**, and **cormorants** could be found there. **Hippos** and **crocodiles** played along the banks of the Nile as well as in the river itself. Among the fish population were **perch** and **catfish**. **Cats** roamed freely and sometimes lived in Egyptian homes.

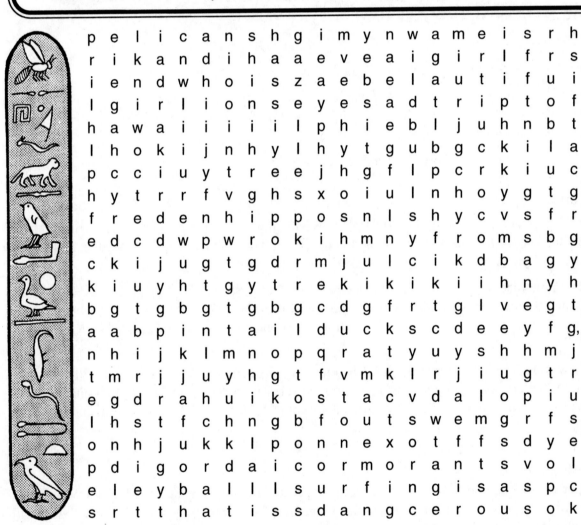

```
p e l i c a n s h g i m y n w a m e i s r h
r i k a n d i h a a e v e a i g i r l f r s
i e n d w h o i s z a e b e l a u t i f u i
l g i r l i o n s e y e s a d t r i p t o f
h a w a i i i i l p h i e b l j u h n b t
l h o k i j n h y l h y t g u b g c k i l a
p c c i u y t r e e j h g f l p c r k i u c
h y t r r f v g h s x o i u l n h o y g t g
f r e d e n h i p p o s n l s h y c v s f r
e d c d w p w r o k i h m n y f r o m s b g
c k i j u g t g d r m j u l c i k d b a g y
k i u y h t g y t r e k i k i i h n y h
b g t g b g t g b g c d g f r t g l v e g t
a a b p i n t a i l d u c k s c d e e y f g,
n h i j k l m n o p q r a t y u y s h h m j
t m r j j u y h g t f v m k l r j i u g t r
e g d r a h u i k o s t a c v d a l o p i u
l h s t f c h n g b f o u t s w e m g r f s
o n h j u k k l p o n n e x o t f f s d y e
p d i g o r d a i c o r m o r a n t s v o l
e l e y b a l l l s u r f i n g i s a s p c
s r t t h a t i s s d a n g e r o u s o k
```

Internet Extender

Wild Egypt

gttp://touregypt.net/wildegypt/index.htm

Activity Summary: Follow this online safari to tour the Nile, as well as the land and Red Sea, through great pictures and captions at this Web site.

Ancient Egypt and Science

Before beginning any of the science projects below, provide the students with some background information about the Egyptians' many contributions to modern society. Establish the following facts:

- The 24-hour day and the calendar based on the sun were both developed by the Egyptians.
- The study of angles and geometry is based on information learned from the Egyptians.
- The scientific study of medicine began in Egypt.
- Egyptian picture writing has links with the Japanese and Chinese forms of graphics.
- The development of papyrus made recorded knowledge in books a possibility.
- Egyptians were pioneers in irrigation and agriculture.

Papyrus

- Outline the steps for making papyrus in a flow chart.
- Make paper or "papyrus" using tissue paper. For materials and directions see the book *Paper by Kids* by Arnold E. Grummer (Dillon Press, Inc., 1990) or *50 Simple Things Kids Can Do To Save the Earth* by the Earthworks Group (Andrews and McMeel, 1990).
- What is papyrus? Write a short paragraph describing this plant. Draw a picture of it.

Simple Tools

- Ancient Egyptians were the first to use a plow. What simple machine is a plow? Construct a chart to show the six simple machines—inclined plane, lever, wheel and axle, pulley, wedge, and screw. Describe and then draw a picture of each one.
- Which simple machines did the Egyptians employ in the construction of the pyramids? How would the construction process have been different if the wheel and axle or the pulley had been available to them? (For background information about machines, see Teacher Created Materials' *Simple Machines*, #227.)
- Mortar was used to help reduce friction when moving large stones. What is friction? When is it helpful? What are some applications of friction in everyday life? (For more information about friction, see *Introduction to Physics* by Amanda Kent and Alan Ward, Usborne Publishing, Ltd., 1990.)

Preservation

- Egyptians embalmed bodies to preserve them. Experiment with preservation. Place a fresh pickle in a jar of salt water. Slice another fresh pickle in half; place it on a paper towel. Predict what will happen to the pickles. Record your observations for at least one week. Compare the observations with the predictions.
- Preserve some fruit or vegetables. Invite the home economics teacher to demonstrate how some foods can be preserved. Discuss other preservation methods.
- Go to a grocery store. Make a list of all the foods that have been preserved.

About the Nile

Supply groups with the following background information. Have them complete the six levels of questions.

For centuries the Nile remained an obscure and unknown river. Even its earliest inhabitants didn't know the source of its mighty waters. Not until rather recent (mid-1800s) British explorations did its myriad secrets surface. It is now known that the Nile is 4,200 miles or 6,720 kilometers long—making it the longest river in the world. The source of these waters lies at Jinja in the north shore of Lake Victoria. As it flows northward in a convoluted route, it drops thousands of feet along the way until it reaches its final destination, the Mediterranean Sea.

Even though its source may have been unknown for centuries, the Egyptians took full advantage of the Nile River. People were able to live secure in the knowledge that they were safe from intruders who didn't dare cross the deserts that surrounded their fertile valleys. Because of the annual flooding, the Egyptians were able to establish a fairly regular cycle of planting and harvesting. Excess crops were then exported, making Egypt a wealthy nation. Animals thrived in the waters and surrounding land of the Nile. Goods were easily transported on barges and ferries. Probably the most valuable gift of the Nile was papyrus, a tall reed which grew along its banks. Papyrus was used to make paper, and Egypt was the sole supplier of this product until rag paper was invented in the twelfth century.

Knowledge

Write a list of eight facts from the text. Draw a picture of the Nile, its convoluted route, and its final destination.

Comprehension

Retell in your own words how the Egyptians utilized the Nile to their advantage. Write a paragraph that tells what is now known about the Nile River; use your own words.

Application

Why was papyrus so significant for the Egyptians? Draw and illustrate some typical events that occurred on the Nile.

Analysis

Write five words from the paragraphs above that can be used to describe the Nile River. Characterize the Nile, using words and phrases from the text.

Synthesis

Write three new titles for the text that would indicate what it's about. Create a poster to advertise the text so others will want to read it.

Evaluation

What is the most important idea presented in these two paragraphs?

Pyramid Cross Section

Carefully examine the cross section of the pyramid. Use your observations, the book *Pyramid*, and other resources to answer the questions.

Questions

1. What room leads into the True Burial Chambers?
2. How tall is the Grand Gallery?
3. What material is used to fill in the bottom of the pyramid?
4. What is the function of the Small Pyramid?
5. Where is the pharaoh's boat buried?
6. What is the Causeway?
7. How was the roof of the burial chamber supported?
8. What structure topped the pyramid?
9. Where is the pharaoh's coffin?
10. Why was the Entry covered over?
11. How did workmen get out of the pyramid?
12. When were the Granite seals placed in the Grand Gallery's corridor?
13. Of what material were the pyramid stones composed?
14. What was the purpose of the False Burial Chamber?
15. Why is this cross section useful?

On Your Own

- Draw and label a cross section of a simple machine or a building.
- Write a glossary for this cross section.
- Which would be easier to read: a cross section or a flat diagram? Defend your choice.

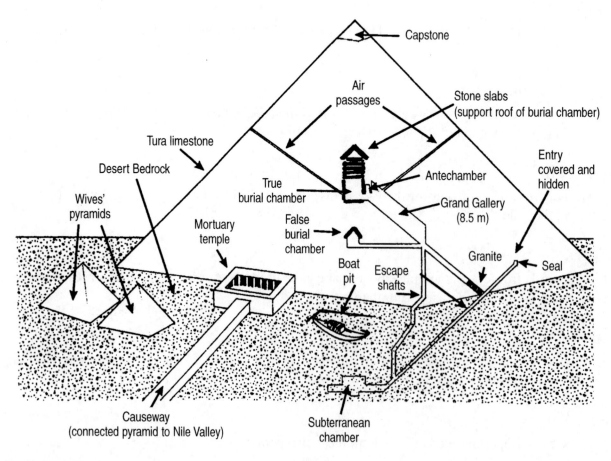

Research Topics

The study of ancient Egypt unearths an abundant source of interesting research topics. Assign the following activities as individual, paired, or grouped projects.

- Write your name in hieroglyphs. It's easy with *The Scribe*, an interactive computer program for Apple computers. The video was developed by the Department of Education of the Detroit Institute of Arts, 5200 Woodward, Detroit, MI 48202. Support it with the book *Egyptian Hieroglyphics for Everyone* by Joseph and Lenore Scott (Crowell, 1968).

- Play and learn about Egypt at the same time. The Learning Company has a new program (for ages 10 and up) called *Challenge of Ancient Egypt*. It is made for IBM and compatibles which are listed on the box.

- Read and discuss *The Riddle of the Sphinx from Classic Myths to Read Aloud* compiled by William F. Russell, Ed. D., Crown Publishers, 1989. Write your own riddle story about another Egyptian phenomenon.

- Find out how the Egyptians gathered natron. Explain how this compound was used in the mummification process.

- Explain how the geography of the Nile River made the pharaoh's control over his people a relatively easy task.

- Make a three-dimensional model of a pyramid. Use plaster of Paris, clay, mud, or any other medium that would be appropriate.

- Research how paper is made today. Compare the process with the Egyptian method of making papyrus. Construct a chart or Venn diagram of your findings.

- Make a list of all the animals that were indigenous or native to Egypt. Tell how the Egyptians felt about each one. For example, hippos were pests because they trampled crops and could also capsize boats. Hunters would try to spear them to death.

- Draw a chart showing all the goods and products that Egypt imported and exported.

- List the gods that the Egyptians worshiped. Draw a picture of each one and explain the function of each.

- The pharaoh wore different crowns for different occasions. Describe and write about each.

- Learn how to play senet. Make up your own game using a game board, markers, and throwing sticks. Write directions for your game and teach others how to play.

- Make a time line to show the reigns of the pharaohs.

- Finding Tutankhamen's tomb was an archaeological triumph. Defend this statement. Research Englishman Howard Carter's search for this monument.

- What was the Rosetta stone? Who found it? What was its significance?

- Read articles about Egypt. Some periodicals to look through include *World, Faces, Cricket,* and *National Geographic*. (See the bibliography on page 80 for more information.)

An Egyptian Feast

Although ancient Egyptians did not enjoy the vast variety of foods available now, they did have a healthful diet. Favorite foods included dates; figs; grapes; honey; and flat, coarse bread. In addition, Egyptian farmers grew onions, leeks, garlic, beans, lettuce, lentils, barley, cucumbers, melons, and gourds. Meat and poultry included ducks, geese, gazelle, pigs, sheep, and goats. Beer and wine were common beverages. The only thing lacking in their diet was citrus fruit—lemons, oranges, limes, etc.

Prepare some Egyptian foods as a class. Then have a food-tasting party. Serve grape juice to drink. Check the recipe below and the Internet Extender Web sites for many more possibilities.

Date Nut Bars

Ingredients: 1 cup (240 mL) chopped dates; ⅔ cup boiling water; 1 teaspoon vanilla; 2 eggs; ½ cup butter or margarine; 1 cup (240 mL) brown sugar; ¼ teaspoon salt; 1 teaspoon baking powder; 1 tablespoon cocoa; 1⅔ cups flour; 1 cup (240 mL) chopped walnuts (optional)

Directions

- Mix dates and boiling water in a bowl; let stand for 15 minutes.

- In another bowl, beat butter and sugar; add eggs.

- Combine flour, salt, baking powder, and cocoa with butter, sugar, and eggs.

- Mix in the dates with water and walnuts.

- Spread on a greased cookie sheet and bake 25 minutes at 350°F (180°C).

- Cool and cut into bars.

Internet Extender

Food in Ancient Egypt

http://www.geocities.com/~amenhotep/glossary/food.html

Activity Summary: Read about the types of food eaten by the ancient Egyptians and compare it to what we eat today.

Egyptian Recipe Page

http://touregypt.net/recipes/

Activity Summary: This Web site has a list of 18 recipes for Egyptian foods. Select several of these to print and then have the students prepare them.

Archaeology on the Net

Internet Extenders

Visit the following Web sites to learn about exciting past and present archaeological digs.

Rosetta Stone

http://www.british-museum.ac.uk/egyptian/EA/index.html

Summary: The Rosetta Stone is now in the British Museum. This Web page describes what it is, when it was found, and its significance. Click on "What Does the Rosetta Stone Say?" to find an English translation of the text, as well as the history behind its being written.

King Tut

http://guardians.net/egypt/tut1.htm

Summary: This excellent Web site offers information and pictures regarding the exciting discovery of Tutankhamen, the boy king. After reading the introduction and looking at the photographs, scroll down to the list of links. Click on "Howard Carter's Journal" and read his record of this discovery, especially on February 25–27 as he first opened the sealed chamber. Other links lead to more of the story of Tut, including his life and early death.

The Mummy of Tutankhamen

http://www.geocities.com/~amenhotep/mummy/catalog_royal/tutankhamun.html

Summary: This outstanding Web site has a thorough and exciting description of the contents of the famous tomb, the discoveries about the mummy, and the history of King Tut. Great illustrations are provided that bring this story to life.

Treasures of the Sunken City

http://www.pbs.org/wgbh/nova/sunken/

Summary: This Web site is based on a NOVA program about the underwater discovery and excavation of the fabled site of Pharaoh's Lighthouse, one of the Seven Wonders of the Ancient World. Learn about this underwater dig and the discovery of such treasures as a huge statue of Ptolemy, 26 sphinxes, and some obelisks. A teacher's guide for a related lesson on this dig is included at this Web site.

Excavations by the British Museum

http://www.british-museum.ac.uk/egyptian/EA/index.html

Summary: This Web site leads to information about three recent excavations in Egypt—El Ashmunein, Tell el-Balamun, and Sudan. These may be accessed by clicking on the names of these areas on the map of Egypt, which is also at this Web site.

Restoring the Great Pyramid

http://guardians.net/hawass/restoregp.htm

Summary: Visit this Web site to see photographs and information about how the Great Pyramid was recently restored to correct the problems caused by too many tourists.

Technology Extenders

The following technology extenders are suggestions the teacher may use to reinforce the content learning of this unit with computer technology experience. Each activity is designed to involve the student in the merging of technology and the subject matter of this thematic unit.

1. **Software:** any paint, draw, and graphics program
   Activity—*Pyramid Power:* Using line, shape, color, and paint tools, design and print out an Egyptian pyramid filled with items a pharaoh might have had entombed with him for his trip to the afterlife. Several copies can be made, cut out, and glued together for a 3-D pyramid with each face showing different objects. These may later be cut out and used as 3-D jigsaw puzzles.

2. **Software:** any database program with a software suite such as *ClarisWorks*, etc.
   Activity—*It's About Time:* Create a database to chronicle important dates and events in the history of ancient Egypt. Sample items might include the following:

   a. *Date:* 4000 B.C.   *Event:* Settlement begins along the Nile.

   b. *Date:* 3100 B.C.   *Event:* Upper and Lower Egypt are united under one king.

   c. *Date:* 3000 B.C.   *Event:* Hieroglyphics are invented.

3. **Software:** any spreadsheet program, such as those included in *ClarisWorks*, *Office*, etc.
   Activity—*Nile Valley Flood Cycle:* After gathering information about the Nile and its cycles, students compare the months of the year, the high and low levels of the river, flood season, planting season, and harvest season. Show them how to log these into the cells of a spreadsheet and print the information. Help them learn how the computer will convert this information into various bar graphs and pie charts.

4. **Software:** any desktop publishing program, such as the *Print Shop*, *Publisher*, etc.
   Activity—*Howard Carter Wants You!* Have students use their knowledge of Howard Carter's expeditions for the secret lost tomb of King Tutankhamen to create a poster on the computer. The poster should advertise for help in the adventure. Have them emphasize romance, adventure, bravery, exotic locale, wealth, and fame. Humor ("Hints from Howard," "Tips from Tut"), hieroglyphics, and ancient Egyptian illustrations can all be a part of this project. Print, share, and display.

5. **Software:** any desktop publishing or word processing program
   Activity—*The Curse of King Tut:* After discussing the legend of the curse placed on anyone who disturbed this tomb (and the eerie death of Lord Carnarvon), have pairs of students work together to write a play about the opening of Tut's tomb and its aftermath. Use "Egyptian-looking fonts, borders, and patterns to write the script and design playbills.

6. **Software:** *HyperStudio* or any other multimedia program
   Activity—*Time Traveler:* Have students work in small groups to produce a slide show containing graphics, narration, sound, animation, and text on life in ancient Egypt. A time traveler journeys back to ancient Egypt and observes the daily lives of the people, returns to the present to tell us of Pharaoh's duties and family, rites of death, mummification, and the afterlife; the priests' customs and gods; the classes of kings, priests, artisans, and farmers.

7. **Software:** *HyperStudio* or any other multimedia program
   Activity—*Famous Pharaohs:* Have students in small groups prepare multimedia reports on rulers and their exploits, such as Akhnaton (*monotheism*), Hatshepsut (*wise female leader with a false beard*), Ramses (*great building projects*), Zoser (*first real pyramid*), and Thutmose III (*extended the empire*). Include names, dates of reigns, and significant accomplishments.

Using the Pages Wisely

Because of economic, environmental, and educational concerns, paper and copymachine usage have come under scrutiny. Therefore, some simple solutions have been compiled and outlined below for your use.

1. Whenever possible present the work orally. Even though there are a number of worksheets throughout this book, many can easily be presented as an oral exercise. For example, for the activity on page 13, copy the word bank on the chalkboard or overhead projector for all to view. Explain the directions to the students. Decide if you want them to answer orally or in writing before you begin reading the sentences.

2. Convert workbook pages into overhead transparencies. Some schools have the proper equipment for this process, but if yours doesn't, many copy centers are equipped to prepare your copies. Afterwards, save your transparencies in labeled manila folders. If desired, you may make a cardboard frame (a cut-up file folder works well, too) for each page. This makes it easy to handle as you place and remove it from the projector.

3. Write directions on the chalkboard or overhead projector. For example, instead of making a copy of the Section Activities (pages 10 and 11) for each student, write the activities and direct the students to copy them. Of course, instructions can also be presented orally.

4. You will not need as many copies of a page if you group the students and provide only one copy for each group.

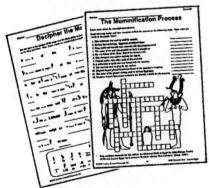

5. After copying a page on a copy machine, glue the sheet to index stock (or copy directly onto the index paper, if available), oaktag, or other paper, and laminate. Students can work directly on the page with water-based, wipe-off pens. Another alternative is to have the students place a sheet of tracing paper over the copy so they can work directly on the paper. Store the laminated worksheets in labeled manila envelopes or folders, or punch holes in the pages and compile them in a loose-leaf notebook.

6. When making copies use both sides of the paper whenever possible. Also, encourage the students to save their one-sided papers in a special collection box. Make new copies on the blank sides of the paper when enough has been collected.

7. Instead of laminating, slip copies into clear plastic sleeves. This serves as protection for the paper, and students can also write on the plastic with wipe-off pens.

8. Choose and use these workbook pages wisely. Not every student will need to complete every page in the units outlined.

King Tut's Mirror
A Bulletin Board

King Tut's mirror was shaped like an ankh, the Egyptian hieroglyph that means life. This simple bulletin board will give students a chance to reflect on life as they study about life in ancient Egypt. Complete directions, purposes, and an illustration can be found below. The pattern for the ankh appears on pages 75 to 77.

Bulletin Board

Materials: black or other dark butcher paper; stapler; scissors; aluminum foil; rubber cement

Directions:

- Line the bulletin board background with butcher paper and staple in place.
- Reproduce the ankh pattern (pages 75 to 77) onto white construction paper.
- Cut out as directed and assemble.
- Cut out an oval of aluminum foil to fit behind the ankh.
- Attach the foil paper ankh to the rubber cement.
- Staple to the bulletin board background.
- Write a title for the bulletin board directly onto the background. Use white chalk and draw block or stylized letters (see diagram below).
- Use the bulletin board for any of the purposes outlined.

Purposes:

- Display the bulletin board before you begin your studies. It will captivate student interest, and they will be anxious to learn more.

- Direct the students to pretend they are King Tut as they look into the mirror. Have them write a story about what they see.

- Use the mirror for the "Picasso" art project on page 22.

Lettering Hints

- On a strip of tagboard or construction paper, write the title in block letters. Use a thick or broad-tipped marking pen.

- Paint on the letters with a medium brush and tempera paints.

- Use letter stencils.

- Print large letters. Intersperse them with dots (see diagram).

REFLECT

King Tut's Mirror *(cont.)*
A Bulletin Board

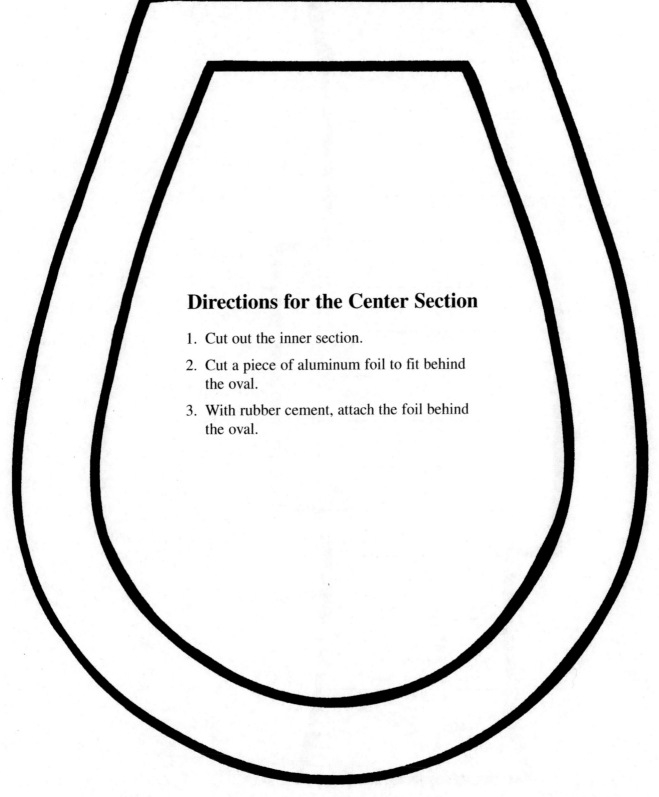

Directions for the Center Section

1. Cut out the inner section.

2. Cut a piece of aluminum foil to fit behind the oval.

3. With rubber cement, attach the foil behind the oval.

King Tut's Mirror *(cont.)*
Bulletin Board

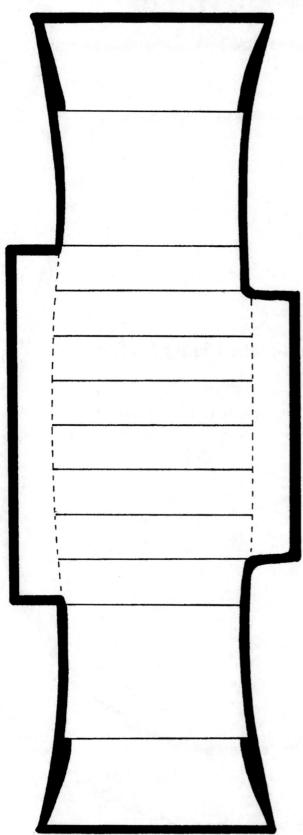

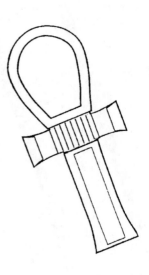

King Tut's Mirror
Bulletin Board *(cont.)*

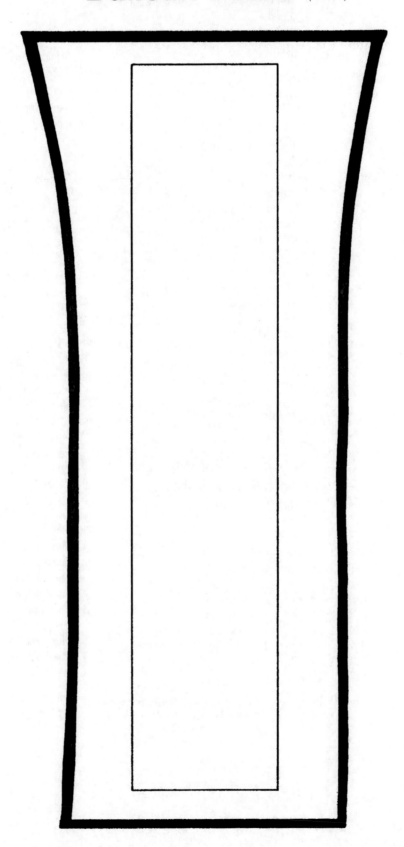

Answer Key

page 9
Egypt Map

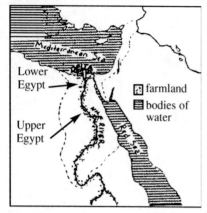

Lower Egypt

Upper Egypt

☑ farmland
☰ bodies of water

page 13
1. sarcophagus
2. canopic jars
3. mummification
4. dolerite
5. inundation
6. pharaohs
7. temenos wall
8. ba
9. resin
10. porticullises
11. plumbline
11. plumbline
12. alabaster
13. capstone
14. mastaba
15. ka

page 17
1. The land…
2. Scribes prepared…
3. Work orders…
4. Tunnels were dug…
5. Each block…
6. The men…
7. The stone block…
8. The work gang's…

page 18
Funerary Complex

Temenos Wall

This 30 foot wall surrounded the base of the pyramid for protection from intruders

Boat Pit

The funeral barge was buried here

Causeway

The covered passageway connected the Valley Temple to the Mortuary Temple

Pyramid

Its function was to provide a safe burial structure for the pharaoh

Mortuary Temple

Ceremonies were performed here before the pharaoh's body was buried in the pyraimid

Valley Temple

The pharaoh's body was first brought here

page 19
1. 480 ft/146 m
2. 9/12 = ¾
3. 1,900 years
4. 2,000
5. 2,960 ft/1,000 m
6. 10 mo.
7. 5
8. 7
9. 2,000,000
10. 960 km
11. 124
12. 2,443

page 26
1. Great Pyramid
2. lion
3. Ramses the Great
4. to be weighed in afterlife
5. Black
6. Boris Karloff
7. Anubis
8. world underneath Earth
9. 20 years
10. henna
11. False
12. all of them
13. khuzza lawizza
14. linen
15. Nile River, Red Sea
16. galena
17. by bartering
18. True
19. Figs, dates, grapes
20. It didn't grow there.

page 27
One of the seven wonders of the ancient world is the pyramid of Khufu at Giza.

page 29
1. beeswax
2. animals

page 29 (cont.)
3. gold
4. Imsety
5. Osiris
6. natron
7. cartonnage
8. *Book of the Dead*
9. linen
10. amulets
11. hieroglyphs
11. habits

page 32

Name	Location	When Built	Description
The Pyramids	Egypt	2600 B.C. to 1000 B.C.	Tombs built for Egyptian kings
Hanging Gardens	Babylon	between 605 and 562 B.C.	gardens laid out on brick terrace 75 feet above the ground
Colossus	Rhodes	early 200s B.C.	huge bronze statue of the god Apollo
Temple of Artemis	Ephesus	about 550 B.C.	huge marble temple with wood-tile-covered roof
Lighthouse of Alexandria	Egypt	between 283-246 B.C.	guided ships into the city's harbor
Statue of Zeus	Olympia, Greece	about 435 B.C.	gold and ivory statue of Zeus
Mausoleum	Halicarnassus	about 350 B.C.	huge white marble tomb

page 46
(These are suggested answers; answers may vary.)
1. accumulated; fascinating; tombs; pharaohs; pyramids; monoliths; exotic
2. scurried; soul; ducked; alley; Egypt
3. stacked; teetered; pale
4. tattered; incense; fragrant; curled
5. ceremony; sacrificial; procession

page 49
1. Melanie hides them.
2. They join the gang.
3. They throw them over the fence.
4. They make him Pharaoh.
5. They stay indoors and make costumes.
6. They ask her to play Nefertiti.
7. They decide not to ask more questions.

Answer Key *(cont.)*

page 50

1. 2, 1, 3
2. 2, 1, 3
3. 3, 2, 1
4. 1, 2, 3
5. 3, 1, 2
6. 1, 3, 2
7. 2, 3, 1
8. 3, 2, 1

page 51

page 52

1. Professor
2. Casa Rosada
3. Mrs. Ross
4. Mr. Schmitt's cousin
5. Elizabeth
6. April
7. Ken
8. Melanie
9. Caroline
10. Toby
11. Security
12. Marshall
13. Dorothea
14. Mr. Bodler
15. Mr. Ross

page 53

1. frame of mind
2. biggestwheels
3. going off your rockers
4. trimming the new kid down to size
5. off the hook
6. cracking up
7. out from underfoot
8. get her teeth into
9. go jump off the bridge
10. bunch of chickens
11. copout
12. dig it
Explanations may vary.

page 54

1. Bes
2. Khoum
3. Sobek
4. Taweret
5. Nekhbet
6. Khepri
7. Sekhmet
8. Meretseyer

page 58

1. N
2. C
3. C
4. C
5. N
6. C
7. N
8. N
9. C
10. C
11. N
12. C
13. N
14. N
15. C

page 61

page 62

1. mouse
2. mule
3. fox
4. eel
5. pig
6. owl
7. lamb
8. ox
9. bee
10. ant
11. elephant
12. Iark

1. eats tiny amounts
2. you're in trouble
3. stop; slow down
4. he's clumsy
5. it's pouring
6. she's very angry
7. take the lead
8. town is quite small

page 63

a. 𓈖𓈖𓈖𓏥𓏥𓏤𓏤𓏤
b. 𓈖𓈖𓈖𓏥𓏥𓏥𓈖𓈖𓏤𓏤𓏤
c. 𓆓𓈖𓈖𓏤
d. 𓈖𓏥𓏥𓏥𓈖𓈖𓈖𓏤
e. 𓈖𓈖𓈖𓏥𓏥𓈖𓈖
f. 𓈖𓈖𓏤𓏤𓏤
g. 𓆓𓏥𓈖𓈖
h. 𓏥𓏥𓈖𓈖𓈖𓏤𓏤

page 65

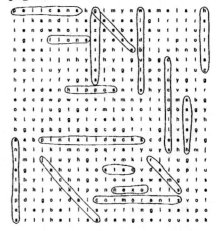

Cats - Bastet   Hippos-Seth
Crocodiles-Sobek   Cows-Hathor
Rams - Amun-Re   Jackals-Anubis
Cats because Bastet was daughter of
sun god Re-she represented power of
sun to ripen crops. Hippos were
dangerous because they could easily
overturn their papyrus boats.

page 67

Knowledge: Check answers for
accuracy. Comprehension: Check work
for accuracy. Application: They were
the sole suppliers to all of the ancient
world; check drawings.

Analysis: Obscure, unknown, mighty,
long, longest, convoluted; long, flows
northward, 4,200 m long, obscure and
unknown, full of myriad secrets, has a
convoluted route, drops, thousands of
feet. Synthesis: Check answers for
accuracy. Evaluation: Although the
Nile was obscure and unknown to the
rest of the world, the Egyptians used it
to their advantage.

page 68

1. ante chamber
2. 8½m
3. desert bedrock
4. burial place of pharaoh's wife
5. boat pit
6. corridor connecting pyramid to Nile
7. stoneslabs
8. capstone
9. True Burial Chamber
10. so no one would steal contents
11. escape shaft
12. after pharaoh's burial
13. Tura limestone
14. to mislead would be thieves
15. helps visualize how pyramids are built

Bibliography

Fiction

Budge, E.A. Wallis, translator. *The Book of the Dead.* University Books, 1990.

Carter, Dorothy. *His Majesty, Queen Hatsheput.* Lippincott, 1987.

Climo, Shirley. *The Egyptian Cinderella.* Harper, 1989.

Green, Roger. *Tales of Ancient Egypt.* Penguin, 1972.

Manniche, Lise. *The Prince Who Knew His Fate.* Putnam, 1982.

McGraw, Eloise. *Mara, Daughter of the Nile* Penguin, 1985.

Snyder, Zilpha Keatley. *The Egypt Game.* Dell, 1967.

Stolz, Mary. *Cat in the Mirror.* Dell, 1978.

Nonfiction

Aliki. *Mummies Made in Egypt.* Harper Trophy, 1979.

Allan, Tony. *Pharaohs and Pyramids.* Usborne Publishing, 1977.

Cohen, Daniel. *Ancient Egypt.* Doubleday 1990 and The Tomb Robbers. McGraw Hill, 1980.

Cork, Barbara and Struan Reid. *The Young Scientist Book of Archaeology.* EDC Publishing, 1987.

Gibling, James Cross. *The Riddle of the Rosetta Stone: Key to Ancient Egypt.* Harper Collins, 1990.

Hart, George, *Ancient Egypt.* Alfred A. Knopf, 1990 (an Eyewitness Book) and *Exploring the Past. Ancient Egypt.* HBJ, 1988.

Ions, Veronica. *Egyptian Mythology.* Peter Bedrick Books, 1983.

Knight, Joan. *Journey Into Egypt.* Viking Kestrel, 1986.

Macaulay, David. *Pyramid.* Houghton Mifflin, 1975.

Oliphant, Margaret. *The Egyptian World.* Warwick Press, 1989.

Perl, Lila. *Mummies, Tombs and Treasures.* Clarion, 1987.

Porell, Bruce. *Digging the Past.* Addison Wesley, 1979.

Reiff, Stephanie Ann. *Secrets of Tut's Tomb and the Pyramids.* Raintree Children's Books, 1977.

Vornholt, John. *Mummies.* Avon, 1991.

Watson, Phillip J. *Costume of Ancient Egypt.* Chelsea House, 1987.

Woods, Geraldine. *Science in Ancient Egypt.* Franklin Watts, 1988.

Young, Caroline. *Castles, Pyramids and Palace.* Usborne, 1989.

Periodicals

"Ancient Egyptians Dances" by C. Mullen. *Cricket.* Jan. 1988, pages 48–50.

"The Gold of the Pharaohs" by R.S. Bianchi. *Faces.* Dec. 1989, pages 12–15.

"Kingdom of Kush and Riddle of the Pyramid Boats." *National Geographic.* April, 1988.

"Mummy Making: The Why and How." *World.* June, 1990, pages 14–15.

"The Rediscovery of Ancient Egypt" by E. Payne. *Cricket.* Sept. 1991, pages 12–16.

Teacher Created Materials

TCM137—*Newspaper Reporters*

TCM227—*Simple Machines*

TCM318—*Literature and Critical Thinking: Mystery* (contains *The Egypt Game*)

TCM759—*Hippo Shape Note Pad*